On Eagles' Wings:
An Exploration of Eucatastrophe in Tolkien's Fantasy

By Anna Thayer

Text Copyright © 2016 Anna E. Thayer
Cover Illustration © Jay Johnstone 2016

First published, 2016 by Luna Press Publishing, Edinburgh

On Eagles' Wings: An Exploration of Eucatastrophe in Tolkien's Fantasy
© 2016 Anna E. Thayer. All rights reserved. No part of this publication may be reproduced, stored in a retrieval system, or transmitted in any form or by any means, electronic, mechanical, photocopy, recording or otherwise, without prior written permission of the publisher. Nor can it be circulated in any form of binding or cover other than that in which it is published and without similar condition including this condition being imposed on a subsequent purchaser.

www.lunapresspublishing.com

ISBN-13: 978-1-911143-07-9

CONTENTS

Abbreviations   iv

Preface   v

Slow-Kindled Courage. A Study of Heroes in the Works of J.R.R. Tolkien   1

Spiritual Mimesis: The Lord of the Rings   19

Moving Mandos: The Dynamics of Subcreation in 'Of Beren and Lúthien'   29

Seeing Fire and Sword, or Refining Hobbits   53

Clean Earth to Till: A Tolkienian Vision of War   73

Stars Above a Dark Tor: Tolkien and Romanticism   93

A Star Above the Mast: Tolkien, Faërie and the Great Escape   111

An Old Light Rekindled: Tolkien's Influence on Fantasy   129

ABBREVIATIONS

The Lord of the Rings	*LotR*
The Fellowship of the Ring	*FotR*
The Two Towers	*TT*
The Return of the King	*RotK*
The Hobbit	*TH*
The Silmarillion	*TSil*
Unfinished Tales of Númenor and Middle-earth	*UT*
On Fairy-Stories	*OFS*
Farmer Giles of Ham	*Giles*
Smith of Wootton Major	*Smith*
The Adventures of Tom Bombadil	*Bombadil*
Bilbo's Last Song	*BLS*
Leaf By Niggle	*LN*

PREFACE

The clouds were torn by the wind, and a red sunset slashed the west. Seeing the sudden gleam in the gloom Bilbo looked round. He gave a great cry: he had seen a sight that made his heart leap, dark shapes small yet majestic against the distant glow.

"The Eagles! The Eagles!" he shouted. "The Eagles are coming!"[1]

If you are at all familiar with Tolkien's work, then Bilbo's cry – proclaiming the arrival of Eagles – will be no stranger to you. Indeed, it is somewhat of a hallmark of the Master of Middle-Earth, one rejoiced over and lampooned in equal measure by both lovers and critics of his writing: at the moment of crisis, the eleventh hour when darkness holds sway and there is nothing more that the heroes can do to win the day, these plot-armoured birds appear, our protagonists fall conveniently unconscious, and when the heroes awake, the good guys have won.

A reductive way of looking at it, perhaps; but the Eagles, and their ability to swoop in and save all at the last possible moment (without a focaliser to witness exactly how they do it) seem, superficially, to fly in the face of good storytelling. You could even argue that they entirely undercut the narrative by making all the efforts of the heroes amount to... well, nothing. And then there's that niggling question – if they had all this power, why in Middle Earth didn't they step in before, and save everyone a good thrashing?

---

1. J.R.R. Tolkien, *The Hobbit*, HarperCollins, London, 1999, first published Allen and Unwin 1937, p. 263. All quotations from *TH* are taken from this edition.

Tolkien was not infallible, either as a man or a storyteller, and while some elements of his mythos resist our attempts to pin them down (Tom Bombadil-o, anyone?), it is possible for us to understand the Eagles – even if we continue to object to them. To do so, we need to look into Tolkien's critical writing and, in particular, his concept of eucatastrophe:

> ...I would say that Tragedy is the true form of Drama, its highest function; but the opposite is true of Fairy-story. Since we do not appear to possess a word that expresses this opposite – I will call it eucatastrophe. The eucatastrophic tale is the true form of fairy-tale, and its highest function... The consolation of fairy-stories, the joy of the happy ending: or more correctly of the good catastrophe, the sudden joyous 'turn'... [the] sudden and miraculous grace: never to be counted on to recur... [gives] a fleeting glimpse of joy, joy beyond the walls of the world... it can give to child or man that hears it... a catch of the breath, a beat and lifting of the heart, near to (or indeed accompanied by) tears... A tale that in any measure succeeds in this point has not wholly failed, whatever flaws it may possess.[2]

Tolkien's treatise as to the purpose and function of fairy-stories is as much a work of theology as it is of literary theory, culminating in his view that those stories that evoke the eucatastrophic turn ultimately reflect what he calls 'the Great Eucatastrophe' (*OFS*, 73): the story of the birth, death and resurrection of Christ, which

---

2. J.R.R. Tolkien, 'On Fairy Stories' in *Tree and Leaf*, HarperCollins, London, 2001, first published Allen and Unwin 1964, pp. 68-69. All quotations from *OFS* are taken from this edition.

is 'the eucatastrophe of Man's history' (*OFS*, 72) – and that the taste of Joy which we experience in fairy in the unlooked for 'turn' is a glimmer and a pointer to that supreme eucatastrophe in our own, primary reality. Tolkien leaves Plato – and his theory of forms – quite in tatters: for Tolkien, story, rather than distracting us from the true nature of things by presenting pale copies and imitations, actually, at its pinnacle, has the potential to draw us closer to God. Better let those poets back into the Republic, Plato!

So how does this concept illuminate the Eagles for us? We need to understand them as a narrative embodiment of Tolkien's eucatastrophic theory; they are the unlooked for grace, the redemptive turn – such a strong glimpse of Joy that the protagonists cannot truly and consciously look on it.

Of course, not being God themselves, the Eagles don't solve everything. Despite their intervention, Thorin still dies, Frodo is still so injured that he cannot remain in Middle Earth. But these aquiline amigos are a pointer to that presence beyond the walls of the world that were so instrumental in Tolkien's life and writing. Perhaps, in choosing the Eagles to crystallise this concept, Tolkien had in the back of his mind a few verses from Isaiah:

> Lift up your eyes and look to the heavens...
> those who hope in the Lord
>   will renew their strength.
> They will soar on wings like eagles;
>   they will run and not grow weary,
>   they will walk and not be faint.[3]

---

3. *The Holy Bible New International Version*, Hodder & Stoughton, London, 2000, *Isaiah* 40, v. 26, 31.

As this preface might suggest, I've been fascinated, inspired and led by Tolkien's concept since childhood. Whatever my line of enquiry into Tolkien's work, the sequence of clues has always led to the same culprit: eucatastrophe. The book that you're holding represents a kind of eucatastrophe casebook, a series of investigations into Tolkien's work that reveal how overarching this theory was in his writing and mindset. It is a theory that has, in turn, enormously influenced my own genesis as a critic and a writer.

I invite you to join me on my journey into the eucatastrophic qualities of Tolkien's stories – for, while it found its pithiest expression in eagles' wings, its touch on the landscape of Middle Earth is entirely inescapable.

Slow-Kindled Courage. A Study of Heroes in the Works of J.R.R. Tolkien[1]

It is posited that in the dislocation between literature's example and reality's experience, the Great War created a backlash against the linguistic and ideological form of heroic literature, eliciting a sense of 'disenchantment' for concurrent poets and writers. Heroes in Tolkien's fictions are examined as an attempt to reinstate these older frameworks of heroism, especially at levels of sophrosynic achievement or Christian mimesis. Discussion covers the historical context of the Great War, models of heroism upon which Tolkien drew, Tolkien's own theory regarding the links between the primary world of history/reality and the secondary world of literature, and the crossing of these issues to elicit the heroes of his fiction. Exploration of Tolkien's heroes illustrates the way in which Tolkien attempts to escape the prevailing disenchantment of his age, but concludes that his heroes are ultimately symptomatic of the time in which he wrote.

> We all have a problem with heroes. We want them
> so badly that we keep inventing new ones.[2]

If literature is a mimetic art, then heroes in literature both reflect and answer the need for heroes in the real world. The *Iliad*, the

---

1. First published in *Tolkien and Modernity Vol. II*, in Frank Weinreich and Thomas Honegger, eds, Walking Tree Publishers, Zurich and Berne, 2006.
2. Colin Burrow, 'Heroes: Saviours, Traitors and Supermen', *The Guardian Review*, 9 October 2004, p. 14.

Aeneid, the Bible, *Beowulf,* historiographic works such as those of Wace or Laʒamon: all exemplify the curious overlap between the secondary world of literature and the primary world of history. This dialogue between reality and fiction is a complex system of encouragement and self-perpetuation for writers and readers alike.

In this article, Tolkien's heroes are examined in terms of their antecedents, the heroic spaces created for them, and the ways in which they enter into the aforementioned dialogue with history via the historical moment of their creation.

FAIRIES AND FUSILIERS

In Tolkien's time history and literature were closely intertwined in creating a model of heroism. Partially due to the amount of literature preserved, the Great War is one of the most-documented conflicts in western history. Generally speaking, the prevailing initial literary voice of the trenches came from officers and soldiers who were themselves educated on epics: the *Iliad*, the *Aeneid*, *Paradise Lost*. These possess a high-linguistic register that praises courage, honour and glorious death in battle, *Paradise Lost* doing so in its Homeric depiction of Satan. The trench-writers applied this style of thought and linguistic expression to a new conflict; for example, Rupert Brook's *Peace* captures a sense of language that originates ideologically in Homer:

> Now God be thanked Who has matched us with His hour
> And Caught our youth, and wakened us from sleeping...
> Glad from a world grown old and cold and weary,
> Leave the sick hearts that honour could not move,
> And half-men, and their dirty songs and dreary,
> And all the little emptiness of love![3]

---

3. John Stallworthy, ed., *The Oxford Book of War Poetry,* Oxford University Press, Oxford, 1984, p. 162.

This elucidation of honour and shame shows war as the ideal occupation of youth. Married to the Homeric framing ('hearts that honour could not move') is a redemptive bellicosity influenced by Christianity: '…we have found release there, / Where there's no ill, no grief…'

But this glorious view was disturbed by the sheer scale of the war; linguistic traits characteristic of the Classics and the Christian faith, used previously to aggrandise battle, were employed to sing a different song:

> What passing bells for these who die as cattle?
> Only the monstrous anger of the guns.
> Only the stuttering rifles' rapid rattle
> Can patter out their hasty orisons.
> No mockeries for them from prayers or bells,
> Nor any voice of mourning save the choirs, –
> The shrill, demented choirs of wailing shells;
> And bugles calling for them from sad shires.[4]

In merging heroic/Christian language, Owen challenges views that automatically confer heroism on war. He does the same in *Strange Meeting*, where the poem's dream-like frame is reminiscent of Odysseus' and Ajax's meeting in Odyssey XI; the title of 'Arms and the Boy' plainly references the *Aeneid*'s opening line, *Arma uirumque cano* ('I sing of arms and of the man'), emphasising soldiers' youth. An archaic linguistic register associated with the values of war is consistently employed to undermine them, for Owen's subject was 'the pity of war', not its heroism.

Siegfried Sassoon wrote likewise. Keenly aware of 'one… who

---

4. Wilfred Owen, 'Anthem for Doomed Youth', in Edmund Blunden, ed., *The Poems of Wilfred Owen*, Chatto and Windus, London, first edition 1931, p.80.

reads/ Of dying heroes and their deathless deeds',[5] his concern was to highlight the bitter difference between perception and reality. *The Hero*, for example, depicts the 'gallant lies' told to keep up heroism's façade for an Every-Woman whose son has been killed. Sassoon was also aware of the point where history, literature and war interlocked. In *Songbooks of the War* he writes:

> In fifty years, when peace outshines
> Remembrance of the battle lines,
> Adventurous lads will sigh and cast
> Proud looks upon the plundered past...
> And dream of lads who fought in France
> And lived in time to share the fun.[6]

These poets sought to reflect the conflict of their time. Given the accepted canon of war poetry, prominently showcasing Owen and Sassoon, it can be said that the anti archaic-language backlash succeeded. That those dying were so young seems however to have turned the tide against more than the classics; this disenchantment of war also lashed out against fairy story:

> The child alone a poet is:
> Spring and fairyland are his...
> Wisdom made him old and wary
> Banishing the Lords of Fairy.
> Wisdom made a breach and battered
> Babylon to bits: she scattered
> To the hedges and the ditches
> All our nursery gnomes and witches...

---

5. Siegfried Sassoon, 'Remorse' in *Collected Poems of Siegfried Sassoon,* Faber and Faber, London, 1961.
6. Op. cit., Collected Poems, pp. 86-7.

None of all the magic hosts,
None remain but a few ghosts
Of timorous heart, to linger on
Weeping for lost Babylon.[7]

Here the advent of wisdom is associated with war ('breach', 'battered', 'ditches'), and the death of faërie. John Garth writes: 'Graves' image of the end of innocence – wisdom scattering the nursery fairies – indicates the literal meaning of disenchantment. The Great War had broken a kind of spell'.[8] The broken spell created a post-world-war anxiety about heroic nature, hitherto defined by Homer, Virgil and the fantastic. 'The Western Front made the fairy aesthetic seem both desperately necessary and hopelessly anachronistic'.[9]

Tolkien, himself a trench-soldier, countered this linguistic and ideological background, offering a divergent approach: his '…real taste for fairy stories was wakened by philology on the threshold of manhood, and quickened to full life by war'.[10] Linguistically and ideologically, Tolkien's writing resounds with archaisms, and in this literary etymology he tries to resurrect the values dethroned by the writings of his contemporaries. In responding to the disregard of heroic language, Tolkien's writing challenges the economy of truth represented by the canon of 'disillusioned' writers like Owen and Sassoon. Tolkien's writing reflects his desire to rekindle a model of heroism despite the trend of history. A childhood friend had remarked to him that as writers they 'had been granted some

---

7. Robert Graves, 'Babylon' in Beryl Graves and Dunstan Ward, eds, *The Complete Poems of Robert Graves,* Heinemann, London, 1916.
8. John Garth, *Tolkien and the Great War: The Threshold of Middle-Earth,* HarperCollins, London, 2003, p.292.
9. Diane Purkiss, cited in Garth (2003:303)
10. J.R.R. Tolkien, 'On Fairy Stories' in *Tree and Leaf*, HarperCollins, London, 2001, first published Allen and Unwin 1964, p. 42.

spark of fire… that was destined to kindle a new light, or, what is the same thing, rekindle an old light in the world.'[11] For Tolkien, this spark resided in the mythopoeic realm of faërie.

PRISONERS AND DESERTERS: TOLKIEN'S THEORY OF FAËRIE

The function and appeal of fairy tales and similarly fantastic stories has long been discussed. Relatively few detailed analyses have been completed, though notable among these are the Brothers Grimm, Propp, Jung, Campbell, C.S.Lewis, Tolkien himself and Bettelheim. All agree that these stories fulfil an important need, although explanations differ. Jung discusses the appeal and function of myth in terms of archetypes (such as the Shadow, the Animus/Anima, and the Syzygy). In *The Uses of Enchantment*, Bettelheim posits that fairy tales give symbolic form to trying situations for children: 'The fairy tale simplifies all situations… Its figures are clearly drawn… All characters are typical rather than unique'.[12] The formative system provided by stories and heroes for children is also examined by Margery Hourihan in *Deconstructing the Hero*.[13] In 'On Fairy Stories', Tolkien states that these tales have a 'prophylactic' effect for adults, whose oversight in critical thought he laments. He describes the main veins of this effect as recovery, escape and consolation, which in turn resolve themselves at their highest point into what he termed 'eucatastrophe'. In his distinctions of these functions, Tolkien asserted that a reader sought stories to escape from the world and recover the means to view it clearly, thereby returning to it renewed. In this he has common ground with writers like Bettelheim, except Tolkien's

---

11. Op. cit. [8], Great War, p. 308.

12. Bruno Bettelheim, *The Uses of Enchantment*, Thames and Hudson, London, 1976, p. 8.

13. Margery Hourihan, *Deconstructing the Hero*, Routledge, London and New York, 1997.

theory is trans-generational. Aware that some critics were quick to call an adult taste for fairy stories escapism or 'juvenile trash',[14] Tolkien used his three-part-theory to distinguish between the 'escape of the prisoner and the flight of the deserter'.[15] The crux of his position was in the fact that after reading, readers returned to the world rather than making a constant withdrawal from it (the act of deserting). That Tolkien uses terms like 'deserter' reflects the conflict of his time, linking war, faërie and theory together. With his theory in mind, it would be reasonable to expect Tolkien's heroes to bring a sense of recovery to his works.

MODELS OF HEROISM: KLEOS AND SOPHROSYNE

Hero-theory runs from ancient Greece to more modern writers like Thomas Carlyle and Lucy Hughes-Hallett. For the purposes of this article, literary heroism is broadly viewed as a bipolar delineation between *kleos* and *sophrosyne*.

Kleos is the Greek word for renown or glory; personal renown is paramount in this heroism. Hughes-Hallett suggests that these heroes are 'superb spirit[s]… associated with courage and integrity and a disdain for the cramping compromises by means of which the unheroic majority live their lives – attributes that are widely considered noble'.[16] The distinction between unheroic majority and hero sets the latter 'higher' than others on the mortal scale; this is suggested by frequently antagonistic roles between heroes and other figures of authority such as kings. The primary example of this hero is Achilles: offered the choice between living a long and comfortable life but having no fame, and going to war, dying

---

14. Edmund Wilson, 'Oo, Those Awful Orcs!' in *The Nation* 182, 1956, p. 312-14.

15. Op. Cit. [10], 'On Fairy Stories', p. 61.

16. Lucy Hughes-Hallett, *Heroes: Saviours, Traitors and Supermen*, HarperCollins, London, p. 1.

young and winning great glory, he chooses the latter.[17]

Not every hero seeking renown falls under Achilles' category. *Kleos* could be further defined as the constant quest for renown (Achilles), the quest for another object (Beowulf or Siegfried), and the romance quest on behalf of a lady (Yvain or Lancelot). Norse and Classical heroes would be concerned with their reputation or their quest, while romance heroes often possess spiritual undertones, especially in the ornate, religiously-inspired modes of address of *fin'amor*.

Opposed to *kleos* is *sophrosyne*, the virtue of heroic temperance. Considered a fatal flaw of excess in tragedy (where it constitutes vital inaction), and often associated with women or the young, it was Christianity during the Mediaeval and Renaissance periods which facilitated the shift towards *sophrosyne* as a heroic virtue. Examples of sophrosynic heroes would be mediaeval hagiographies, Guyon in *The Faërie Queene*, or Milton's Christ in *Paradise Regained*. *Sophrosyne* is '…very difficult to give to a literary hero, because inaction is a highly undramatic mode of behaviour';[18] it necessitates the substitution of psychological/ spiritual action for physical heroics.

These templates highlight a fundamental divide in literature's heroic roles; a *kleos* hero, of noble birth, perhaps divinely-engendered, was predetermined for great things. He was to excel in matters of prowess for his own advancement and glory, or for the honour of his lady. A sophrosynic hero was to imitate a higher standard: Christ. A variation on being divine offspring, the hero was to seek God's glory and will over his own.

This Christian mimetic (heroes mirroring Christ) was certainly

---

17. Homer, *The Iliad*, translated from the Greek by E.V. Rieu, Harmondsworth, 1950, p. 34, verse 339.
18. Richard Douglas Jordan, *The Quiet Hero: Figures of Temperance in Spenser, Donne, Milton and Joyce*, Catholic University of America Press, Washington, 1989, p. 4.

one that Tolkien strove to create; eucatastrophe is defined as:

> 'a piercing glimpse of joy... [that] rends indeed the very web of story... in the 'eucatastrophe' we see in a brief vision that the answer may be greater – it may be a far-off gleam or echo of *evangelium* in the real world... The Great Eucatastrophe, the Christian joy is... high and joyous. Because this story is supreme; and it is true. Art has been verified. God is the Lord, of angels, and of men – and of elves. Legend and history have met and fused.'[19]

Tolkien calls this the 'true form of fairy tale...its highest function.'[20] Thus we may assume that Tolkien's heroes should enter the heroic tradition at a level which corresponds to the Christian one. The modern hero is a fusing of *kleos* and *sophrosyne*; he must act morally and often exhibit physical prowess, but only when vital. Like the trench-soldiers, he is an unheroic figure in a heroic circumstance. That Tolkien chooses to write in the sophrosynic tradition opposes this view.

Tolkien's stance was not unique; *On Fairy Stories* and eucatastrophe were fermented in the creative arena of the Inklings, a group of Oxonians who met regularly to translate Norse sagas and read each others' work. Other Inklings included C.S.Lewis and Charles Williams: their works (e.g. *The Cosmic Trilogy, The Chronicles of Narnia, War In Heaven, The Greater Trumps*) all exhibit the same 'Christianised' theory of the relation of story/story-telling to the real world. In Williams' fictions, for example, characters come to learn that the super-spiritual bubbles away intensely within the bounds of the world in which they live. In the

---

19. Op. cit. [10], 'On Fairy Stories', p. 71-3.
20. Op. cit. [10], 'On Fairy Stories', p. 68.

autobiographical *Surprised By Joy*, C.S.Lewis states that the joy he has been describing would be called 'eucatastrophe' by Tolkien. As in his youth, Tolkien was involved with a group of writers that sought to influence the world. By accenting the spiritual in their writings, these writers presented fictitious framings of Ephesians 6:12: '...for we wrestle not against flesh and blood, but against principalities, against powers, against the rulers of darkness of this world, against spiritual wickedness in high places'.[21] Interestingly, this Pauline letter then applies the topoic motions of arming the epic hero to Christians:

> Stand, therefore, having your loins girt about with truth, and having on the breastplate of righteousness; and your feet shod with the preparation of the gospel of peace; Above all, taking the shield of faith, wherewith ye shall be able to quench all the fiery darts of the wicked. And take the helmet of salvation, and the sword of the Spirit, which is the word of God. (*Ephesians* 6:14-17)

This makes the Christian a hero with an epic level of prowess – but, as *sophrosyne* dictates, it is a spiritual prowess.

Tolkien's Heroes

Tolkien's heroes draw on the traditions outlined above, his scheme of heroism modulating as his writing progresses and exhibits different heroic spaces. Considered here are Beren and Túrin in *The Silmarillion*; Bilbo in *The Hobbit*; Aragorn and Frodo in *The Lord of the Rings*. Tolkien was engaged in depicting heroism for

---

21. *King James Bible*, Robert Barker, first published London, 1611. All quotations from the *King James Bible* are taken from this edition

a culture sung increasingly in disillusion. If, as Aldous Huxley observes, 'civilisation has absolutely no need of nobility or heroism',[22] the question is what Tolkien's heroes – written for the superficially anti-heroic modern reader of the post-war critical environment – reflect of his time.

BEREN AND TÚRIN: A BACKWARD GLANCE?

In *Modern Heroism*, Robert Sale suggests that for Tolkien, *The Silmarillion* is 'a nostalgic glance...back to a world he would much rather have lived in'.[23] Sale asks how Tolkien can create heroes of an older tradition as a modern author, and hints at the Great War when he says: 'If despair is created by the sense that History has overwhelmed the world, then the heroism will be created in defiance of that same history'.[24] Because Tolkien-as-author feels the pressure of history, Beren and Túrin feel it too. Despite his fictional setting, Tolkien's content points to his modern position.

A synopsis of Beren's heroism evokes a romance quest; he has to claim one of the Silmarils from the Iron Crown of Morgoth, deliver it to King Thingol, and thereafter claim the hand of Lúthien, whom he loves. But the story also operates on a darker level; the Silmarils carry a dreadful curse into which many have already been drawn; Beren is a stranger at court, dispossessed and the last of his people. Lúthien is an elf who must give up her immortality for Beren. Unusually active for a woman in a romance, she refuses to be left behind by Beren and the narrative follows her in as much detail as it does Beren.

Tolkien was obviously aware of this measure in heroics whose

---

22. Aldous Huxley, cited in Roger Sale, *Modern Heroism : Essays on D.H. Lawrence, William Empson and J.R.R. Tolkien,* University of California Press, Berkley, 1973, p. 1.
23. Op. cit., Modern Heroism, p. 228.
24. Op. cit., Modern Heroism, p. 11.

balancing unbalances the romance-quest. Lúthien belongs to a tradition of prominent women that goes back to Marie de France, Chrétien de Troyes and later Spenser. But unlike Spenser's handling of Una and Redcrosse, Tolkien cannot balance his narrative in a fashion appropriate to his genre. Attempting to re-confine his heroine, Tolkien gives Lúthien a hound as companion who defeats Sauron and battles with Morgoth's wolf at the tale's end. Nevertheless, Lúthien is made conspicuous by her heroism. She rescues Beren from Sauron, sings Morgoth to sleep (facilitating the seizure of the Silmarils), heals Beren more than once, and pleads for his life to be returned to him in the Halls of the Dead. But Lúthien is not of Britomart's class; her prowess is not in arms.

The story counterpoises Beren's doom and Lúthien's voice; Lúthien consistently tips the possession of heroic status towards herself. Beren is weighed down by the grief of his humanity, but Lúthien, in her constant active role, is an artist within the tale who directly affects its ending. In persuading the divine agents, the Valar, to grant Beren his life, she becomes what Tolkien would call a 'sub-creator'; a position conferred upon her by her voice, which originates in her elven descent and connection therein to faërie. Faërie is a world with which Beren, fashioned by 'doom', cannot compete.

This extra-literary weight on the text is created by the author's position in history; the narrative is skewed between the typical hero-of-the-sword, and the artistic heroism of language figured in Lúthien. For example, there is more awe in the text when Huan the hound speaks (linguistic heroism) than when he wrestles with Carcaroth (physical heroism). When Beren names Lúthien *Tinúviel*, he establishes the romance element of the narrative in foregrounding his love for her. But in the same breath he surrenders his position as hero to her by ceding to linguistic-heroism: 'Then the spell of silence fell from Beren, and he called to her, crying

Tinúviel; and the woods echoed her name'.[25] Beren's surrender of narrative and heroic primacy began when he entered the woods that were the realm of the Elves; here the woods themselves confirm that the silence of physical heroism is to be replaced by the voice.

The dominance of Lúthien's heroism is asserted at the tale's end when conclusion itself is tackled:

> The song of Lúthien before Mandos was the song most fair that ever in words was woven, and the song most sorrowful that ever the world shall hear... and Mandos was moved to pity, who never before was so moved, nor has been since (*TSil*, 220).

The narrator also writes: 'Thus [with Beren's death] ended the Quest of the Silmaril; but the Lay of Leithian, Release from Bondage, does not end' (*TSil*, 220). Tolkien acknowledges the dualism of the heroism in his story, a conflict that lies in interweaving several modes and heroes into one story. What reflections does a tale where the artist (Lúthien) is more overtly heroic cast upon the narrator? At its outset, the narrator tells us that what we are reading is 'told in fewer words' than older versions and 'without song' (*TSil*, 189), pointing to the fact that the story-teller has little grasp of the tale's principal heroic ethic, words. But is this to give more space to Lúthien? Does the narrator's alignment with linguistic heroism explain why Beren's physical heroism seems less important? Downplaying the narrator's own craft may reflect the fact that Lúthien, primary exponent of the faërie heroism of tongue, is 'now lost' (*TSil*, 221). The dehabilitation of the narrator in the loss of faërie suggests the literary losses incurred in the

---

25. J.R.R. Tolkien, *The Silmarillion*, ed. Christopher Tolkien, HarperCollins, London, first published Allen and Unwin 1977, p. 193. All quotations from *TSil* are taken from this edition.

disenchantment of Tolkien's contemporaries.

The power attributed to language in *The Silmarillion* reflects Tolkien's love of philology. Robert M. Adams observes: 'Tolkien has a fascination with names... that will probably seem excessive to anyone whose favourite light reading is not the first book of Chronicles'.[26] For example, Túrin's story begins: 'Rían, daughter of Belegund, was the wife of Huor, son of Galdor; and she was wedded to him two months before he went with Húrin his brother to the Nirnaeth Arnoediad' (*TSil*, 235). The Biblical comparison is further evidenced in Tolkien's love of family trees, shown in the *Silmarillion* and the Appendices to *The Lord of the Rings*. The tale of Túrin Turambar is filled with names and the act of naming. One may assert this to be an extension of faërie heroism: power in words equals power in names.

Throughout 'Beren and Lúthien', Beren is accorded names befitting his deeds e.g. Erchamion ('One Hand') or Camlost ('The Empty-Handed'). These create a progressive heroic identity; though not making Beren heroic, they reflect his achieved heroism. Compare this to Genesis 17 or 35, where Abram and Jacob both have their names changed *post factum* to reflect their new status: Abram ('Exalted Father') becomes Abraham ('Father of Many') when he commits himself to God, and Jacob (figuratively 'He deceives') becomes Israel ('He struggles with God').

Túrin names himself, and frequently the event eliciting this naming is one he has falsely interpreted, as when he names himself Neithan ('The Wronged') refusing the king's pardon 'in the pride of his heart'. The sheer volume of names (seven in all) attributed to Túrin in the narrative bear witness to his attempt to mould his own heroism. Túrin is overshadowed by Beren – 'This man is not

---

26. Robert M. Adams, 'The Hobbit Habit' in N.D. Isaacs and R.A. Zimbardo, eds, *Tolkien: New Critical Perspectives*, Kentucky, 1981, p. 169.

Beren – a dark doom lies on him!' (*TSil,* 251), and in response he reaches for a way to turn himself into a hero.

Túrin's final name, Turambar ('Master of Doom') is a hubristic self-sentence. Empowered by the names he has given himself, Túrin tries to assert authority over the narrator of the text as well as the characters within it when he states that he has mastered his 'dark doom'. Unlike Beren, who accepts his doom, Túrin constantly pulls away from it in his act of naming, and in doing so only succeeds in becoming stuck fast. As a result, Túrin's story feels strongly governed by *wyrd:* the Norse fate. Ironically, Beren receives life for accepting his doom; Túrin receives death resisting it at every turn. Though Beren's strategy may be more 'Christian', it does not reward him with eternal life as a Biblical parallel might suggest; in this, Beren reflects the culture of disillusionment and foreshadows Frodo.

Both Beren and Túrin struggle in their heroic spaces because they are created 'backwards' as insertions into a tradition long passed. Beren and Túrin are forgeries, albeit intelligent ones. As a modern Christian, Tolkien cannot help but create characters that cannot quite sup with Achilles or Beowulf. This is exemplified in Túrin's encounter with Glaurung the dragon: while Túrin's literary predecessor, Siegfried, slew the dragon and claimed his prize, Túrin falls prey to Glaurung's voice, and as a consequence loses everything. Glaurung acknowledges Túrin's *kleos*-naming when he goads him: 'Then surely in scorn they will name thee, if thou spurnest this gift' (*TSil,* 256). It is Túrin's future reputation that Glaurung manipulates. In steering Túrin from the rescue of Finduilas (a romance quest), Glaurung denies Túrin the chance to become the hero of another genre. In this single moment, Túrin fails to belong either to the heroic genre (by discerning the dragon's guile as Siegfried with Fáfnir), or the romantic one. The result is a tragic matrix that ends with Túrin marrying his sister, and with both their deaths.

Beren and Túrin exemplify key aspects of Tolkien's heroic scheme; clearly language, name and deed all have a part to play in framing a hero. Epic, Norse and Mediaeval traditions were part of his thinking, and the Middle-earth of *The Silmarillion* provides a place where these heroes can exist. *The Silmarillion* explores heroic temperament, with his heroes' fate as the first residue of war's disenchantment, for the heroism of Middle-earth's heroes is never questioned. When Tolkien began to write *The Hobbit* in the 1930s, Middle-earth's heroic space changed to accommodate the new protagonists.

BILBO BAGGINS: A 'MODERN' HERO

'In a hole in the ground there lived a hobbit';[27] so begins Tolkien's first published fiction. Middle-earth has changed; *The Silmarillion*'s narrator would not write this way, nor would his heroes live in such a hole, even if it 'mean[t] comfort' (*TH,* 3). But in essence the author's premise remains; emphasis in the opening words is not on defining what a hobbit is, but a detailed description of where one lives. Middle-earth is still an arena fashioned for its heroes, though the shift in tone and locale alerts us to the shift in hero. Hobbiton is not a heroic setting, and Bagginses 'never [have] any adventures or [do] anything unexpected' (*TH*, 3). The narrator tells us that this story will be about one who breaks away from that mould: 'He may have lost the neighbours' respect, but he gained – well, you will see whether he gained anything in the end' (*TH,* 4). This is an active invitation to consider the hero's achievements.

Bilbo is defined as stereotypical of the English upper-middle-class (with emphasis on decorum and social niceties); we are

---

27. J.R.R. Tolkien, *The Hobbit*, HarperCollins, London, 1999, first published Allen and Unwin 1937, p. 3. All quotations from *TH* are taken from this edition.

asked to weigh his 'fame' at home against the fame achieved in his quest. In this sense, Bilbo is anti-heroic. He is anti-heroic also in being neither wise nor strong, but hired as a burglar. Conducted by dwarves (who, with the almost concurrent appearance of Walt Disney's *Snow White*, may not have been viewed seriously), the quest would have no place in 'epic' literature. Although the dispossessed dwarves hold the quest highly, 'a journey from which some of us, perhaps all of us, may never return', (*TH*, 17), Bilbo does not appreciate its epic quality (at the thought of not returning, he faints), and the reader may therefore be less inclined to. A character like Bombur is clearly not designed for the epic tradition. Tolkien initially creates a miniature epic world, and carefully expands it until it becomes a full-blown mythological canvas seen through the eyes of an anti-mythic character.

This distinction is demonstrated in Bilbo's progression from bumbling protagonist to hero: in rescuing the dwarves from the spiders in Mirkwood or Thranduil's dungeons, the hobbit is drawn into heroic circumstances. The reader expects the conversation with Smaug to be the work's climax; it is certainly envisioned as such by the questing characters. That the story does not end with the slaying of the dragon indicates movement from fairy-tale to mythic canvas; but Bilbo retains a common sense that curtails him from either faërie or epic heroism. His unconsciousness at the Battle of the Five Armies reflects his dislocation in the narrative. Bilbo's heroism reaches its height when he relinquishes the Arkenstone to Bard:

> "I hope you will find it useful."
> The Elvenking looked at Bilbo with a new wonder. "Bilbo Baggins!" he said. "You are more worthy to wear the armour of elf-princes than many that have looked more comely in it." (*TH*, 251)

Here Tolkien highlights and reconciles the incongruity he has cultivated throughout the work. Much of the tale's humour stems from Bilbo's anachronism, the unheroic character in a heroic world. In the above quotation, the two are conflated so that the reader sees that as Bilbo can be measured on the scale of Elven-princes he is not such a misfit hero after all. Tolkien does similarly with Thorin's final words:

> There is more in you of good than you know, child of the kindly West. Some courage and some wisdom, blended in measure. If more of us valued food and cheer and song above hoarded gold, it would be a merrier world. (*TH*, 266)

Here Bilbo is not so much affirmed into the heroic tradition as made equal to it in what he loves. However, upon his return to Hobbiton, he has 'lost his reputation… he was no longer quite respectable' (*TH*, 278). Affirmation of heroic equity can pass from mythic to non-mythic, but not from the non-mythic to the mythic: Achilles may dub a trench-soldier heroic, but the trench-soldier cannot claim it for himself. Bilbo comes from the later arm of the sophrosynic tradition; he is a 'moral' hero, who acts when it is right to do so, rather than not acting at all. Nothing he does is for fame or reputation, although this is the way in which he is then measured. *The Hobbit* reflects the perception of reputation and heroism that had been shifted and confused by the Great War; within the frame of children's story Tolkien touches on the concerns of disenchantment and problems for a modern hero.

Spiritual Mimesis: The Lord of the Rings

Tolkien staunchly stated that *The Lord of the Rings*[28] was not an allegory, and that he 'much prefer[ed] history, true or feigned, with its varied applicability to the thought and experience of the reader'.[29] In this regard, *LotR* seems to present itself as historiography; this fused ground of history and myth allows Tolkien to attempt to mirror the spiritual realm in his literature. Tolkien's most prominent heroes, Frodo and Aragorn, are sophrosynic heroes reflecting two aspects of Christ; servant and king. Like Bilbo, they are anachronistic: although in narrative terms they prefigure Christ, in the author's terms they are His descendants. As mimetic heroes, they imitate Christ rather than seeking their own glory, though in this imitation, particularly Frodo's imitation, *LotR* also grapples more with eucatastrophe and disenchantment than Tolkien's earlier works.

Structurally, it is suggested that Frodo and Aragorn are flip sides of the same coin. C.S.Lewis observes: 'All the time we know that the fate of the world depends far more upon the small movement than on the great.'[30] Tolkien's interweaving of plot in *The Two Towers* and *The Return of the King* is highly complex, and Lewis' comment highlights the way in which heroism is split between Frodo and Aragorn accordingly. As a returning king, Aragorn inherits the *kleos* tradition, succeeding Beren and Túrin. In his love for Arwen he explicitly replays Beren's story; like Beren and Túrin he has many names.

---

28. J.R.R. Tolkien, *The Lord of the Rings*, HarperCollins, London, 1995, first published in one volume 1968. All quotations from *LotR* are taken from this edition.

29. Op. cit., *LotR*, Forward to the Second Edition.

30. C.S. Lewis, 'The Dethronement of Power' in Neil D. Isaacs and Rose A. Zimbardo, eds, *Tolkien and the Critics*, Notre Dame, Indiana, 1970, p. 13.

One may easily point to Aragorn and claim that Tolkien is reframing the Arthur myth: Aragorn has a magic sword, comparable in its Elven-craft to Calibeorn in Laʒamon's *Brut*. Caught in a love triangle (between Eówyn and Arwen), Aragorn is the true but unknown king of Gondor, who with a wizard's help regains his throne. At this level the resemblance is striking, but Aragorn is far more modern than Malory's or Tennyson's Arthur. As king he is the story's figurehead, though he bows under the role's weight. In history and legend, kings are expected to be steadfast and wise in their decisions. Literature excels at highlighting instances where they are not (Homer's Agammemnon, Shakespeare's Lear). Within the frame of *LotR* we are aware of kings who failed at crucial times (Isildur).

Both author and Aragorn are aware of this burden, and as a result Aragorn is defined by the crisis of choice: 'I am not Gandalf, and though I have tried to bear his part, I do not know what design or hope he had for this hour, if indeed he had any…' (*LotR,* 387); 'All that I have done today has gone amiss… What is to be done now?… An evil choice is now before us.'(*LotR*, p.404-5). Unlike Túrin, Aragorn is concerned that he makes the right choice for the sake of his heart rather than his historical reputation, 'my heart sees clearly at last', (*LotR*, 409). Aragorn's progressing desire to perform his role affects his names. He begins as Strider; in 'The Council of Elrond' he is announced by his proper name, Aragorn (*LotR*, 240); in 'Farewell to Lórien' Galadriel says 'In this hour take the name that was foretold for you, Elessar, the Elfstone of the house of Elendil!' (*LotR*, 366). Aragorn receives names according to his destiny; only in accepting his right to choice does he announce himself by his own names:

> "I am Aragorn, son of Arathorn, and am called Elessar, the Elfstone, Dunadan, the heir of Isildur Elendil's son of Gondor. Here

> is the Sword that was Broken and is forged again! Will you aid me or thwart me? Choose swiftly!"
>
> [Aragorn] seemed to have grown in stature while Éomer had shrunk; and in his living face they caught a brief vision of the power and majesty of the kings of stone. For a moment it seemed to the eyes of Legolas that a white flame flickered on the brows of Aragorn like a shining crown. (*RotK*, 243)

Aragorn's claim to his heroic space engenders a tier of three responses; first, growth in stature, both literally and metaphorically. Second, a 'vision of power and majesty' that links him historically with previous kings. Only Legolas sees the 'white flame…like a shining crown'. This may be a simple foreshadowing of the crown that Aragorn will wear. In Middle-earth, the Elves are continuously associated with the spiritual level, and Legolas alone sees a reflection of this realm. The flame is comparable to the prophetic fire encircling Iulus' head at the close of *Aeneid II*, or the gospels' account of the dove descending on Jesus at his baptism. Aragorn is spiritually empowered to fulfil his role.

Aragorn is also defined antithetically by Denethor. A steward, not a king, Denethor refuses to relinquish his power. Like Aragorn, he embodies the matrix formed by power and choice, but is associated with a 'fey' mood, and destructive linguistic visions surround him:

> We will burn like heathen kings before ever a ship sailed hither from the West. The West has failed. (*LotR*, 807)

In correspondence with a spiritual heroism modelled on

Ephesians, where Aragorn represents the kingly side of Christ as a hero, that this is the only place in the text where 'heathen' appears is of note. In conjunction with the association of 'the West' with Christendom in literature, this suggests that Denethor represents those who will not imitate Christ in dispensing their power. This is supported by the scriptural resonance of *The Return of the King*, title of the final book.

What distinguishes between Aragorn and Frodo? W.H. Auden wrote: 'One type [of quest hero] resembles the hero of Epic; his superior *arete* is manifest to all... The other type, so common in fairy tales, is the hero whose *arete* is concealed'.[31] While Aragorn claims his *arete* in the text, Frodo laments the right bestowed upon him, 'I wish it had never, never, been found', (*LotR*, 891). His heroism is in his acceptance of his role, even though he is not a king and no great glory will follow. Unlike Bilbo, Frodo is more than a moral hero; the text is riddled with suggestions that providence has chosen Frodo to destroy the Ring: 'Behind that there was something else at work, beyond any design of the Ringmaker...you...were meant to have it' (*LotR*, 55). When Frodo takes the task we are told:

> At last with an effort he spoke, and wondered
> to hear his own words, as if some other will
> was using his small voice.
> "I will take the Ring," he said. (*LotR*, 263-4)

Frodo has constantly to choose to serve; he is empowered to do that in part by providence, in part by his own inclination towards courtesy. Both facets mesh when he spares Gollum, a deed performed out of pity. Frodo is defined like Aeneas in terms

---

31. W.H. Auden, 'The Quest Hero' in in Neil D. Isaacs and Rose A. Zimbardo, eds, *Tolkien and the Critics*, Notre Dame, Indiana, 1970, p. 46.

of his *pietas* (his right-choosing), and like Gawain in terms of his courtesy; he is frequently referred to as a 'courteous halfling', and even astounds Galadriel, 'here she has met her match in courtesy', (*LotR*, 356). It is in Frodo that imitative spiritual heroism is most clearly expressed in *LotR*. While Aragorn has the re-forged Andúril, Frodo's key possession is the phial of Galadriel, whose purpose accents the spiritual level of his quest: 'May it be a light to you in dark places, when all other lights go out' (*LotR*, 367). This echoes Psalm 27: 'The Lord is my light and my salvation'.

Like Aragorn, Frodo is seen at moments 'as though in a vision', again suggesting the spiritual ethic that permeates the fabric of the text. When Frodo spares Gollum, we read:

> For a moment it appeared to Sam that his master had grown and Gollum had shrunk: a tall stern shadow, a mighty lord who hid his brightness in grey cloud, and at his feet a little whining dog. (*LotR*, p.604)

Again one character shrinks while the other seems taller; as with Aragorn, the comparison affirms Frodo's heroic status. Frodo is a truly sophrosynic hero; but as the Ring grows in power it stifles his ability to choose: 'Lead me! As long as you've got any hope left…I'll just plod along after you' (*LotR*, 907). The arena shifts from one visible to the reader to an all-encompassing spiritual one:

> No image of moon or star are left to me. I am naked in the dark, Sam, and there is no veil now between me and the wheel of fire. I begin to see it even with my waking eyes, and all else fades. (*LotR*, 916)

The spiritual is intensely physical for Frodo, but the reader sees only what Sam sees: 'Anxiously Sam had noted how his master's left hand would often be raised as if to ward off a blow, or to screen his eyes from a dreadful Eye that sought to look in them' (*LotR*, 914). Tolkien both highlights and undercuts the unfolding heroism; he distances the reader by giving psychological action viewed second-hand, but closes the gap in giving Sam's vision of the spiritual realm. When Gollum and Frodo meet again after Shelob's lair, Sam's vision sets the scene for Mt Doom:

> Then suddenly...Sam saw these two rivals with other vision. A crouching shape, scarcely more than the shadow of a living thing, a creature now wholly ruined and defeated, yet filled with hideous lust and rage; and before it stood stern, untouchable now by pity, a figure robed in white, but at its breast it held a wheel of fire. (*LotR*, 922)

The key phrase here is 'untouchable now by pity': as Frodo's primary tool in his heroism of right-choosing, this manifold failure of pity distorts his heroic right to choice. The language of free will is inverted at Mt Doom to show its crucial failure: 'I do not choose now to do what I came to do. I will not do this deed. The Ring is mine!' (*LotR*, 924). Here Frodo's legacy of right-choosing serves him; Gollum, whom he had spared, bites off the Ring and falls into the chasm, destroying it and saving his master. In this way right-choosing makes Gollum an agent of eucatastrophe, and allows him to keep his apparently irreconcilable promises to both serve Frodo and seize the Ring. Even in failure, Frodo's choice brings good. Here, eucatastrophe provides Tolkien's *felix culpa*, theoretically relieving the tale of disenchantment in this climax to its spiritual dimensions.

The spiritual nature of Frodo's growth is underlined by his treatment of Saruman back in the Shire:

> I do not wish him to be slain in this evil mood.
> He was great once, of a kind that we should not
> dare to raise our hand against. He is fallen, and
> his cure is beyond us; but I would still spare
> him, in the hope that he may find it. (*LotR*, 996)

Like Milton's Christ in *Paradise Regained*, Frodo returns 'unobserved' to his home; but he does not achieve the same quiet heroism. Christ sacrificially gave his life; Frodo, as Tolkien writes 'thought that he had given his life in sacrifice: he expected to die very soon, and one can observe the disquiet growing in him'.[32] Frodo cannot be a complete hero; he cannot become a king like Aragorn; like Bilbo he receives no recognition in his own country. Frodo's heroism makes no sense without Christ as a comparative, but Christ has not yet appeared in Middle-earth; to be robbed of an adequate heroic comparison cultivates Frodo's disillusion regarding his own deeds; the Shire is saved, 'but not for [him]' (*LotR*, 1006). The sense of enchantment reinstated at Mt Doom slides towards disenchantment in Frodo's 'disquiet', just as the literature of Tolkien's time slides from Homer to Owen when story and reality do not mesh.

False Heroism

It is clear that Tolkien considered heroism carefully; in that consideration he did not ignore concerns, shared with other writers, regarding the effects of literature's heroic depictions. In *LotR* characters are caught between the appeal of *kleos* and the author's decision to write based on *sophroysne*; the Ring tempts characters with this dichotomy: Boromir sees himself leading an

---

32. Humphrey Carpenter, ed., *The Letters of J.R.R. Tolkien*, with the assistance of Christopher Tolkien, HarperCollins, London, 1995, first published 1981, p. 327.

army to overthrow Sauron. Éowyn's love for Aragorn is 'only a shadow and a thought: a hope of glory and great deeds, and lands far from the fields of Rohan' (*LotR*, 849). This false love of heroism brings neither escape nor consolation – she 'goes seeking death' (*LotR*, 823). Sam's internal dialogue in *The Choices of Master Samwise* exemplifies the conflict between Tolkien's heroism of right-choosing and literature's established heroic tradition. On finding Frodo apparently dead Sam considers canonically heroic responses: committing suicide and seeking vengeance. We can assume that these are founded on a reading of literature as Sam makes constant reference to song and story. Deciding to take the Ring he sees a group of Orcs coming towards his master's body. Again, he is afflicted by what he feels is expected of a hero:

> How many can I kill before they get me? They'll see the flame of my sword as soon as I draw it, and they'll get me sooner or later. I wonder if any song will ever mention it: How Samwise fell in the High Pass and made a wall of bodies round his master. No, no song. Of course not, for the Ring'll be found, and there'll be no more songs. I can't help it… I can't be their Ring-bearer. Not without Mr. Frodo. (*LotR*, 718)

Ultimately Sam's choice is not based on literature's dictates but on love for his master. In an interesting turn the height of his heroism, typified by love and service, inspires him to make his own song at the Tower of Cirith Ungol; later he becomes one of the 'chroniclers' of the story itself. Tolkien implies that heroes enchanted by Christian love and 'good' heroic literature become the next generation of artists; Sam's 'visions' (see above) accent his integration with the spiritual realm of Middle-earth. Unlike

Frodo, Sam returns to the Shire at peace and enriched. In these senses, he exemplifies Tolkien's ideas of recovery and mimesis. But, despite the apparent culmination of his theory in Sam, it is in Frodo's position that Tolkien finds himself.

THE DISENCHANTED?

The hero-anxiety engendered by the Great War created a literary environment in which traditional concepts of heroism could no longer match the experience of the primary world. But there was still a need for heroes, one that Tolkien answered by exploring the nature of heroism to disperse the prevailing sentiment of disenchantment. To do this, his writings drew from a large linguistic, literary, religious and historical tradition. Tolkien's heroes try to reinstate heroic vision whilst remaining aware of the dangers of their media.

Charles Douie asked if 'the prose and poetry of this age [were] to be charged with disillusion and despair?'.[33] While Tolkien's theories sought to show that it did not need to be, his greatest hero, Frodo, is beset by disenchantment within and without the text; in Tolkien's historical perspective and in the imminent departure of the Elves, representing the disenchantment of Middle-earth. Frodo's circumstance— caught between the heroic and the unheroic— is a motif of Tolkien's present, a summation of the Great War's disillusioning effect. In this regard, whilst epitomising so much of Tolkien's anti-disenchantment theory, Frodo is inescapably symptomatic of the conflict which he was framed to address.

---

33. Op. cit. [8], Great War, p. 303.

Moving Mandos: The Dynamics of Subcreation in 'Of Beren and Lúthien'[1]

This paper posits that Tolkien's theory of eucatastrophe, expressed tangibly in the workings of The Lord of the Rings, is also powerfully framed in The Silmarillion. In particular 'Of Beren and Lúthien' sustains a debate on the nature of subcreation and the way in which it can be integrated into the primary world of history through the performative acts of oath and song. The culmination of this is seen in Lúthien's song before Mandos, where the eucatastrophic 'second chance' given to the lovers in the primary, historical world is effected by a song reflecting the eternal. Although a short chapter in a longer work, 'Of Beren and Lúthien' charts a complex map detailing the ways that subcreation, here represented by oaths and songs, though always derived from the impulse of the same creative act, can diverge, bringing either eucatastrophe or dyscatastrophe in its wake. This paper also examines the effect of the loss of Lúthien, the tale's primary agent of eucatastrophe, and the way in which this loss ultimately affects the telling of tale itself.

> ...Though all the crannies of the world we filled...
> 'twas our right (used or misused).
> The right has not decayed.
> We make still by the law in which we're made...
> And stir the unseen with a throbbing string.[2]

These lines from the poem *Mythopoeia* indicate the form of

---

[1]. First published in *The Silmarillion: 30 Years On*, Allan Turner, ed., Jena, 2007.

[2]. J.R.R. Tolkien, 'On Fairy Stories' in *Tree and Leaf*, HarperCollins, London, 2001, first published Allen and Unwin 1964, pp. 87-9.

Tolkien's contribution to the critical debate on the interrelation between the eternal, primary, and secondary worlds. Tolkien argues that just as God made men, so men, fashioned in the likeness of God, make still because their fibre retains some consciousness of that initial creative act. Where Tolkien diverges from much of the critical thought preceding him is in asserting that the secondary world, the subcreation of man as represented in poetry, song and prose, can powerfully reflect the essence of the Creator.

He argued that the land of faërie was uniquely suited to this eucatastrophic mimesis, presenting a stage whereon a glimpse of eternal joy could be performed without negating the very real possibilities of failure and sorrow.

The dynamics of subcreation, or the relations between and effects of performative utterances on and in the historical and eternal worlds, are set out at length by Tolkien in 'On Fairy Stories'[3], where these dynamics highlight the contrasting natures of eucatastrophe and dyscatastrophe.

This paper posits that Tolkien's theory of eucatastrophe, expressed tangibly in the workings of *The Lord of the Rings*, is also powerfully framed in *The Silmarillion*. In particular 'Of Beren and Lúthien' sustains a debate on the nature of subcreation and the way in which it can be integrated into the primary world of history through the performative acts of oath and song. The culmination of this is seen in Lúthien's song before Mandos, where the eucatastrophic 'second chance' given to the lovers in the primary, historical world is effected by a song reflecting the eternal. Although a short chapter in a longer work, 'Of Beren and Lúthien' charts a complex map detailing the ways that subcreation, here represented by oaths and songs, though always derived from the impulse of the same creative act, can diverge, bringing either eucatastrophe or dyscatastrophe in its wake.

---

3. Op. cit. [2], 'On Fairy Stories', pp. 1-83.

STRICKING BACK TO THE ETERNAL: TOLKIEN'S FAËRIE

In 'On Fairy Stories', Tolkien reclaims the theories of forms suggested by Plato and twisted almost beyond recognition in the consequent long train of critical debate. Tolkien agrees that there is an eternal, supra-human world, and that the primary or historical world exists below this and that it reflects aspects of that from which it is descended. But, contrary to Plato, Tolkien argues for the innate value of the secondary or created world of artistic endeavour as something that can go beyond the sphere of man and reconnect to the primal, eternal universe. In so doing he explicitly states that story continuously seeks to re-establish the severed link between man and the universe, the great dyscatastrophe of history. Tolkien's theory goes further, stating that the reversal of this severance is achieved in the life of Christ, for:

> ...this story has entered History and the primary world; the desire and aspiration of sub-creation has been raised to the fulfilment of Creation. The birth of Christ is the eucatastrophe of man's history. The Resurrection is the eucatastrophe of the story of the Incarnation.... For the art of it has the supremely convincing tone of Primary Art, that is, of Creation.[4]

In the Christian story, Tolkien argues, creation and subcreation go full-circle. The essence of the power of fairy-stories is that their scope is supremely suited to reflect the same process of despair being replaced by unsought joy, and in so doing to reconnect the reader to the eternal world. Eucatastrophe is when art enables us to grasp the joy of the eternal world.

---

4. Op. cit. [2], 'On Fairy Stories', p. 72.

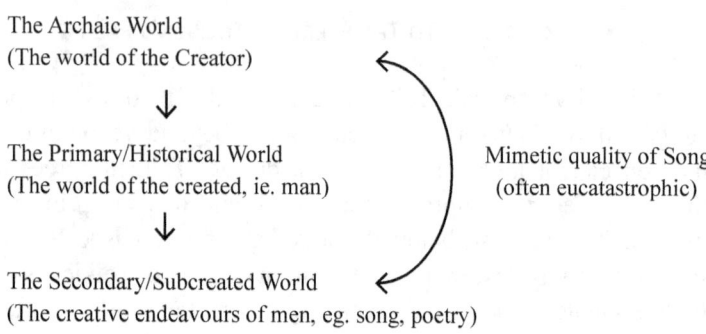

Fig. 1: Tolkien's Theory of Subcreation

THE BEOWULF SYNDROME AND THE EAGLE EFFECT

For scholars and critics, matters would be simplified if Tolkien's works always exemplified this subcreative vision where the text continuously points to the eternal. But as Tolkien himself noted in the preface to the second edition of The Lord of the Rings, he was not writing allegory. For the eucatastrophic to be a credible and effective device, especially in the post- World War era, there had also to be dyscatastrophe. Song needed a minor key to demonstrate the reality of sorrow and failure.

In The Silmarillion this is displayed in the influence of northern mythologies. In tone much of The Silmarillion has about it the notion of labouring under doom, and at times, as in the story of Túrin, this doom is inescapable. The curse lying over the Silmarils is the root of the long defeat that leads to the fading of the elves, and reminds the reader of heroes doomed to failure. This dyscatastrophic 'Beowulf Syndrome', as this paper terms it, is elegiac, and affords the scope to illustrate the tragic potential of man with heart-rending force. Its counterbalance is the 'Eagle Effect', the point where the eucatastrophic vision of the secondary world transcends the text and strikes back to the eternal, momentarily shattering the pervasive mood of its Beowulfian counterpart.

These two textual modes go together throughout Tolkien's works, rising and falling in an ebb and flow which is powerfully reminiscent of the primary world. They work powerfully in The Silmarillion as a whole, especially in the way that oaths and song are counterpoised in 'Of Beren and Lúthien' as both seek to affect the historical world of the text.

To understand a little more about the way these modes are used in 'Of Beren and Lúthien' we first need to consider the textual concept of the eternal world.

THE BALANCE OF THE ETERNAL WORLD

> In the beginning was the Word, and the Word was with God, and the Word was God. He was with God in the beginning. Through him all things were made; without him nothing was made that has been made. In him was life, and that life was the light of men. The light shines in the darkness, but the darkness has not understood it. (*John* 1: 1-5)[5]

The beginning of John's Gospel is a useful departure point for considering the mythology of Middle-earth for several reasons. Firstly, like the book of Genesis and like Eru in 'The Ainulindalë', it attributes considerable power to the spoken word as a thing inherent in and innate to the creator and thus to the eternal. This dynamic gives supernatural value to words, and as such affects the transaction between writer and page, implying that the historical world can be altered by both the utterances and subcreative works of men, just as the creator's voice brought forth the eternal. But

---

5. *The Holy Bible New International Version*, Hodder & Stoughton, London, 1973.

as in many mythologies this scriptural passage also introduces us to the idea that there is opposition in the eternal world, and that the creative moment is not comprehended by the 'dark' quarters who soon attempt to sow discord. The familiar terms of light and dark point to the two figures or groups of power that can be identified in almost any mythology; those that strive for the good, and those that strive for evil. Generally speaking, the forces of good aim to nurture and create, whilst those of evil try to destroy and unlawfully take command of what remains. The creative and destructive both accrue followers of their own, who follow the examples of their masters. In effect, we are left with two groups of 'creators', with one trying to wrest power away from the other.

In Tolkien's work, 'The Ainulindalë' bears the burden of demonstrating the initial conflict between good and evil. It begins by presenting Eru as an unquestionable fact:

> There was Eru, the One, who in Arda is called Ilúvatar; and he made first the Ainur, the Holy Ones, that were the offspring of his thought, and they were with him before aught else was made. (*TSil*, 3)[6]

Eru is placed in prime place at the beginning of this story, and all else is defined against him. This definition is wrought from the outset by identifying the narrator's passive position as a chronicler and setting this against the active verbs that demonstrate Eru's autonomy in creation. Eru makes simply by thinking, paralleling the logos of the Greek gospel of John, and his makings have a chronology that is recounted by the author of 'The Ainulindalë' in such a way that Eru himself cannot be chronicled. Eru is a fact and truth whose own existence and history cannot be described; we hear directly of the making of the Ainur. This indicates that,

---

6. J.R.R. Tolkien, *The Silmarillion*, HarperCollins, London, 1999, first published 1977, p. 3. All quotations from *TSil* are taken from this edition.

much as in the Judaeo-Christian mythos, there is a rift between the created and the creator; the themes of Ilúvatar will be 'played aright' at an unspecified point in the future when all that Eru has created shall 'know the comprehension of each' (*TSil*, 4). By comprehension here the narrator indicates that the created will fully know as they are fully known (compare this with St. Paul's like statement in 1 Corinthians 13:12), and that at this time of full-knowledge discord and dyscatastrophe will be removed.

It comes as little surprise, then, to see that conflict arises through something reaching beyond its part: 'It came into the heart of Melkor to interweave matters of his own imagining that were not in *accord* with the theme of Ilúvatar' (*TSil*, 4, emphasis mine). Here 'The Ainulindalë' is subject to an issue of reception amongst modern readers that it may share with *Paradise Lost*. Surely all Melkor is doing when weaving things of his own thought into the music of the Ainur is facilitating his right to create, a right given to him no less than to any other child of Ilúvatar. Why, then, does this expression lead to him becoming 'dark and terrible'? (*TSil*, 11).

Melkor's self-expression may seem noble, much as Satan's seems to many that study Milton's work. But Melkor's hubristic perseverance in his individuality embodies his arrogance, and is a stepping away from Ilúvatar's theme; he is an agent of discord when he ceases to be 'in accord' with the creator. In so doing Melkor becomes a dissident, creating out of his own mind at a time when it is only his place to be the channel of creative power. He misuses the subcreative responsibility entrusted to him, twisting the theme of Eru away from its intended purpose, and it results in his exile.

The friction between Melkor and the other Valar once on Middle- earth becomes a familiar battlefield between the good of the creator and the destruction of the dissident:

> And they built lands and Melkor destroyed them;

> valleys they delved and Melkor raised them up;
> mountains they carved and Melkor threw them down;
> seas they hollowed and Melkor spilled them; and
> naught might have peace or come to lasting growth,
> for as surely as the Valar began a labour so would
> Melkor undo it or corrupt it. (*TSil*, 12)

It is of note here that Tolkien, in his role as narrator of 'The Ainulindë', chooses a rhythm of words and speech that imitates the half-line balances one might expect to encounter in Anglo-Saxon alliterative verse. For example, we might rearrange the text on the page in the following fashion:

Valleys they delved	and Melkor raised them up;
Mountains they carved	and Melkor threw them down;
Seas they hollowed	and Melkor spilled them

Looking at the text in this way demonstrates the ever-changing impetus that drives the work of the Valar. The destructive strength of Melkor's anti-creation is highlighted; the phrase 'and Melkor' stands like a wall in the centre of each line, seemingly hindering the verse that the narrator strives to create, and yet also becoming a stylistic feature of it. Melkor's own creative efforts, sundered from the creator, are in vain, but he can oppose the other Valar in what they create.

'Of Beren And Lúthien': The Archetypal Tale

The second part of this paper will examine the chapter 'Of Beren and Lúthien' as a remarkably concentrated illustration of the constant interaction of eucatastrophe and dyscatastrophe in a fictional mode which deliberately places them in closer proximity than might be expected in the realistic novel, together with frequent reminders of the power of subcreation, that is to say of the word, within the secondary world itself.

The interaction of eucatastrophe and dyscatastrophe and the differences between subcreation used and abused are highlighted at the beginning of 'Of Beren and Lúthien' in Gorlim's vision of his wife Eilinel. Here the false-creative strength of Melkor is show-cased at a human and primary level: 'There he saw Eilinel, and her face was worn with grief and hunger, and it seemed to him that he heard her voice lamenting that he had forsaken her' (*TSil*, 190). The narrator carefully stresses the insubstantial nature of the vision in using the verb 'seemed'. Gorlim, naturally enough, cries out; 'but even as he cried aloud the light was blown out in the wind; wolves howled, and on his shoulders he felt suddenly the heavy hands of Sauron's hunters. Thus Gorlim was ensnared...' (*TSil*, 190). The false Eilinel, a 'creation' of Melkor's, is nothing more than a phantom, portending death and betrayal. It is blown out by the wind. Contrasting this with Beren's first calling of Lúthien highlights the differences between the true and false creation. Beren's vision of Lúthien is acclaimed by the woods that join him in echoing her name. In these two incidents we see that, much as Frodo will later observe, the creative impulse of evil has the power only to mock the created rather than to make new. Another example of this grisly scope is seen when Beren's dream of carrion-birds sitting over the mere with bloodied beaks is transformed into a mocking reality (*TSil*, 191).

These events bring tragedy into the historical world, and are attributed directly to Melkor. They, along with the description of his efforts against the Valar in 'The Ainulindalë', frame Melkor/Morgoth as a spiteful being with the hubris of Satan and the overwhelming strength of Apollyon.

The conflict between good and evil is then enacted in the

historical world, and moments of eucatastrophe reflect the creator while moments of dyscatastrophe seem to demonstrate the victory of evil at the expense of actors in the historical world. As Tolkien stated, the world of the fairy story is perhaps the only place where this battle can be figured properly, as the setting allows despair and joy better rein than some other genres.

SUBCREATIVE UTTERANCES: OATHTAKERS AND SONGMAKERS

In the Beren and Lúthien story we are presented with two specific forms of subcreation, oath-taking and song-making. Oaths are strongly tied to the weight of the world trammelled by Melkor, while songs are agents of eucatastrophe. By examining the roles played by each in 'of Beren and Lúthien' we are able to watch the tensions between eucatastrophe and dyscatastrophe, and to see how closely the two come together. It is this dualism in the text that ultimately demonstrates eucatastrophe so thoroughly.

We have said that the Middle-earth of Beren's time is one knit-round with mockery and destruction due to Morgoth's power. The driving force behind men in a world ruled by mockery is the binding power of the oath; where mockery pulls apart, an oath binds to a course of action or mode of behaviour. However, oaths are themselves subject to mockery, as Gorlim finds when Sauron promises him that his treachery will be repaid by the restoration of his wife to him. An oath is an indelible utterance that cannot be withdrawn; in response to the mocking birds and the fate that befell his father Beren swears an oath of vengeance, but in so doing must 'forsake' his father's grave. This word, itself of Germanic origin, implies the breaking of another oath; *for* is a negative prefix (as in forbid, fordone), and *sake* in its root comes from an old word meaning legal affairs and duties. The oath creates a future course of action that must be pursued, and, in this sense, we might say that it is the manifestation of the subcreative impulse in a burdened world. A man making an oath is seeking to create or call into the present a future state of being; in Beren's case, to wreak vengeance for the death of his kinsmen. This is a miniature version of the Valar singing Middle-earth into being, for there, also, words fashioned the course of the future. The difference lies in the fact that an oath can only be forged by navigating the web of words which bore it into the world, while song elicits new things. One is drawn, the other is born.

The power of the oath is in its ability to bind the speaker, and the great danger in taking oaths is in breaking them, or taking them lightly. Ironically, the restrictive power of oaths is powerfully demonstrated in Thingol's hall that, as a stronghold of the elves, is a place where we expect song to be at its most powerful. Melian and Lúthien, both associated with the web of the world and subcreation, are either silent or silenced by Thingol. The conflict between Thingol and Beren is emblematic of the tensions between oaths in the historical world; when separate oaths clash there can be no peace between them, as both parties have sworn themselves to a course of action. Thingol and Beren speak with oaths that mock the other, and this mockery ends by tightly tying them both to the fate of the Silmarils; as Melian perceives, Thingol's words have either 'doomed [his] daughter, or [him]self' (*TSil*, 197). The curse of the Silmarils is a historical agent of the Beowulf syndrome throughout the Silmarillion, and Thingol's entrapment in that curse (itself caused by conflicting oaths being made and broken) both literally and metaphorically lengthens the shadows in his kingdom.

The desire for and curse of the Silmarils comes to represent the danger of the subcreated thing misused in the primary world, but also highlights the abiding power in a such a thing. For the Silmarils also hark back to the eternal, and contain within them light from the trees of Valinor. It is of note that in the tale of Beren and Lúthien, the Silmarils are only agents of dyscatastrophe, being wrought about with oaths. The light of the Two Trees will only become an agent of eucatastrophe in *The Lord of the Rings*, when Galadriel gives of the phial bearing 'the light of Earendil' as a gift to Frodo.[7] This demonstrates that it is not the created object itself which is good or evil, but the way in which it is treated by historical actors. In the Silmarils we are reminded again of Morgoth's egotistical pursuit of his own will against Eru's creation. In this way the Silmarils are forerunners of the Ring and link Beren's quest with Frodo's.

Thingol is not the only one whose words are distorted by the web of ill-will surrounding the Silmarils; in Nargothrond Celegorm's oaths to seize the Silmarils inflame rebellion against the rightful King. Finrod, however, refuses to be drawn further into the curse, choosing to keep his oath to aid Beren.

It is in Finrod and the other elves that choose to accompany Beren that we catch a glimpse of the power of an oath kept rightly. Despite his defeat by Sauron, the oaths of Finrod and his company in captivity hold fast in spite of the Werewolf which begins to devour them one by one: 'none betrayed their lord' (*TSil*, 201). None betray their identity of their mission. An oath broken or ill-kept brings mockery and despair, but an oath rightly sustained does not bring hope as we might expect; it brings only the inevitability of doom. Finrod's oath empowers him to 'burst his bonds' when the werewolf comes for Beren, and, typical of a world where glimpses of the eternal are slim, in killing the werewolf he earns his own death. In this act he fulfils his oath and saves his companion, but the redemption of his oath is not marked with any kind of joy or reconciliation:

---

7. J.R.R. Tolkien, *The Lord of the Rings*, HarperCollins, London, 1995, first published in one volume 1968, p. 367. All quotations from *LotR* are taken from this edition.

> "[...] it may be that we shall not meet a second time in death or life, for the fates of our kindred are apart. Farewell!" He died then in the dark, in Tol-in-Gaurhoth, whose great tower he himself had built. Thus King Finrod Felagund, fairest and most beloved of the house of Finwe, redeemed his oath; but Beren mourned beside him in despair. (*TSil*, 204)

The redemption of an oath ends in mourning, just as it does when Beren finally delivers a Silmaril to Thingol. The death of Finrod looks forward to the redemption of Beren's oath to Thingol, and the parting of Beren and Lúthien in grief. The reader feels that in this Beowulfian world where song is suppressed and oaths cannot create any future other than one ending in death, the fate of two lovers caught in the curse of the Silmarils cannot hope to be a happy one.

Songmaking

In a text where the weight of oaths and Melkor's presence are so tangibly figured, the moments of joy represented in song are welcome. An example of this is Beren's first sight of Lúthien. After the darkness of his own journey through lands too terrible for description, this moment is a summer to both reader, narrator and to hero. As with Gorlim's fateful vision, it is evening, and Beren is 'enchanted' (*TSil*, 193). But the evening, a time of fading and deception, is counterbalanced by the 'unfading grass' (*TSil*, 193) and the immediate association of Lúthien with the eternal:

> Blue was her raiment as the unclouded heaven, but her eyes were grey as the starlit evening; her mantle was sewn with golden flowers, but her hair was dark

as the shadows of twilight. As the light upon the
leaves of trees, as the voice of the clear waters, as the
stars over the mists of the world, such was her glory
and her loveliness; and in her face was a shining
light. (*TSil*, 193)

As well as being undeniably the most beautiful of Ilúvatar's children, the narrator here represents in the secondary world (the account we are reading) a historical figure who is undoubtedly an embodiment of the eternal. This tripartite presence from now on dominates the text, granting Lúthien heroic stature in deed and form, a stature often garnered through use of her voice, and her subcreative power. In this sense, she is a kind of eucatastrophe incarnate. When we first see her sing, the narrator shows us how literal the cycle of subcreation is; her song 'released the bonds of winter, and the frozen waters spoke, and flowers sprang from the cold earth where her feet had passed' (*TSil*, 193). Lúthien's voice calls forth things in the physical world, because her voice and presence are manifestations of the first voice that called forth the whole of creation. Beren is enchanted in part because he sees, even if he does not recognise, the eternal world in Lúthien.

It is this vision of the eternal that begins a subcreative process in Beren; 'In his heart he called her Tinuviel, that signifies Nightingale, daughter of twilight, in the grey elven tongue, for he knew no other name for her' (*TSil*, 193). In the absence of absolute knowledge, Beren creates a name for what he has seen, and on hearing her voice 'the spell of silence' (*TSil*, 193) falls from him. His own calling of Lúthien is echoed by the woods – the whole of nature calls her by the name Beren has given her, and Lúthien halts 'in wonder' (*TSil*, 193). It is as though the elven race do not expect to see such a subcreative strain in their mortal brethren, a strain that joins both the eternal and subcreated world. But it also joins them irrevocably to the historical, for it is here that doom falls upon Lúthien, and, struck by the name he gives her, she loves Beren. This complex conflict between the Beowulfian and Eucatastrophic is epitomised by the author when he describes Beren as 'slain by both bliss and grief' (*TSil*,193); where his experience touches near the eternal in loving Lúthien, he reaches beyond a point of ordinary feeling. The sorrow is the dragging weight of the oath-laden historical world in which he is an actor, the bliss an echo of the eternal world for which he longed in creating a name for Lúthien. Lúthien, however, now becomes more deeply meshed into a Beowulfian mode where the oaths surrounding the Silmarils tie her to mortality.

In the power of her song, which will be demonstrated several times in the length of the tale, Lúthien represents the unadulterated strength of the Ea. This makes her a manifestation of Eru's power in Middle-Earth, and gives her an unprecedented skill in song as a subcreative art. The anguish of Beren and Lúthien indicates how in a world filled with false and mocking creation it is difficult to maintain joy. The narrator is always at great lengths to communicate to the reader the brevity of their joy, and in so doing heightens the effect of the Beowulf syndrome.

Apart from Lúthien the tale's other singer is Finrod, whose battle with Sauron in song demonstrates that the eucatastrophe of song is not always enough – especially when it must counter the doom of the Noldor, the oathbreakers. Finrod and Sauron are well matched, and Finrod brings 'the might of Elvenesse' (*TSil*, 201) in his song, figured in the memory of Valinor 'beyond the western world' (*TSil*, 201). But the memory of the kinslaying becomes a powerful movement in the song, and it is this that causes Finrod to fall:

> Then the gloom gathered; the darkness growing
> In Valinor, the red blood flowing

> Beside the Sea, where the Noldor slew
> The Foamriders, and stealing drew
> Their white ships with their white sails
> From lamplit havens. The wind wails,
> The wolf howls. The ravens flee.
> The ice mutters in the mouths of the Sea.
> The captives sad in Angband mourn.
> Thunder rumbles, the fires burn –
> And Finrod fell before the throne. (*TSil*, 201)

In this verse, Finrod's defeat at the hands of Sauron is figured as an inescapable consequence of the curse following the Noldor, who had broken oaths in killing their kin. It is the curse of this broken oath that trammels Finrod's ability to strive in songs more powerful than Sauron's.

Finrod's fall, and following death, are moments that are riven with the consequence of oaths, as we have seen, and the memory of each oath creates a gathering weight on the text that creates a powerful sense of despair, especially in Beren. But it is in this moment that Lúthien arrives, and the power of song is once again underlined:

> In that hour Lúthien came, and standing upon the bridge that led to Sauron's isle she sang a song that no walls of stone could hinder. Beren heard, and he thought that he dreamed; for the stars shone above him, and in the trees nightingales were singing... (*TSil*, 204)

Lúthien's song can loose and bind, turning Beren's prison into a starry world, and frees the captives following Sauron's defeat. But it also redeems the despair of Finrod's death, for his grave remains inviolate 'until the land was changed and broken, and foundered under destroying seas' (*TSil*, 206).

The apocalyptic vision portrayed by the narrator in miniature at Finrod's burial is a forerunner of the song that Beren creates on 'the threshold of the final peril' (*TSil*, 209) as he prepares to descend to Thangorodrim:

> Farewell sweet earth and northern sky,
> For ever blest, since here did lie
> And here with lissom limbs did run
> Beneath the Moon, beneath the Sun,
> Lúthien Tinúviel
> More fair than mortal tongue can tell.
> Though all to ruin fell the world
> And were dissolved and backward hurled
> Unmade into the old abyss,
> Yet were its making good, for this –
> The dusk, the dawn, the earth, the sea –
> That Lúthien for a time should be. (*TSil*, 209-10)

Beren for the first time accounts the world in which he lives good for the fact that Lúthien is in it. Her existence is set on a par with that of the moon, sun, earth and sea, showcasing her as a natural fruit of the creative hand that made them all. This fragment of Beren's song is defiant against the destructive will of Morgoth, and the restrictions of the world in which Beren strives, for Beren here bids farewell to the world and acknowledges simply the beauty and goodness figured in Lúthien. It is a selfless song, and maybe it is this aspect which draws Lúthien so swiftly to him.

THE CONTEST OF OATH AND SONG

We have seen that oath and song perform very different functions in the tale of Beren and Lúthien, but that these functions combine to give a realistic vision of a world trying to fend of dyscatastrophe and seeking hope. This combination of menacing failure and approaching good creates a faërie story in the way that Tolkien envisaged the best of such stories to be. This co-operative between dyscatastrophe and eucatastrophe is highlighted in the climax to the Beren and Lúthien story, where oath and song contest in confronting Morgoth in his hall, a place 'upheld by horror' (*TSil*, 212).

Lúthien's connection to the eternal through her song and her descent from 'divine race' (*TSil*, 212), bring her undaunted before Morgoth. It is her status as an heir of Eru and her beauty which kindle 'an evil lust' (*TSil*, 212) in Morgoth – a desire, the narrator implies, to thoroughly trammel what is in effect the last thing in Middle-Earth which still bears the grace of Eru's creation. The same song which throws all of Morgoth's court into slumber causes the Silmarils to blaze in answer with 'a radiance of white flame' (*TSil*, 213), making the crown in which they are set too heavy for Morgoth's head. It is the power of Lúthien's song that enables the fulfilment of Beren's vow as he cuts a Silmaril from the crown.

It is in this moment of eucatastrophic victory that the tragedy of the tale truly begins: 'It came then into Beren's mind that he would go beyond his vow' (*TSil*, 213). This moment of pride is to have results as severe as those that follow a vow unkept. The court begins to wake, Beren loses both hand and Silmaril to Carcharoth, and Lúthien's failing power is not enough to take them safely from the gates. At the final moment, the pride of an oath exceeded is enough to supersede the hitherto unassailable power of song that Lúthien bears.

Fortuitously, Beren and Lúthien are saved by Eagles who bear them back to Doriath. Though later in Tolkien's work the appearance of eagles will herald being saved from death (as it does for Bilbo in *The Hobbit*, and for all four hobbits in *The Lord of the*

Rings), here their undeniably eucatastrophic presence cannot undo the certainty of death which begins to crowd Beren: 'suffering was graven in his face' (*TSil*, 215). Indeed, the quest of the Silmaril ends in despair, with Beren's death following the fulfilment of his oath to Thingol, and the falling of darkness on Lúthien. In this darkness she goes to the hall of Mandos, and from it comes her last song:

> The song of Lúthien before Mandos was the song most fair that ever in words was woven, and the song most sorrowful that ever the world shall hear. Unchanged, imperishable, it is sung still in Valinor beyond the hearing of the world, and listening the Valar are grieved. For Lúthien wove two themes of words, of the sorrow of the Eldar and the grief of Men, of the Two Kindreds that were made by Ilúvatar to dwell in Arda, the Kingdom of Earth amid the innumerable stars. And as she knelt before him her tears fell upon his feet like rain upon the stones; and Mandos was moved to pity, who never before was so moved, nor has been since. (TSil, 220)

In her final song, it is the grief that Lúthien has come to know in the dyscatastrophic historical world that enables her to move Mandos. Her song, based in grief, both does and does not work eucatastrophe. For Beren and Lúthien are offered the chance to return to the world, but are offered no guarantee of joy. Lúthien's last song speaks of the creation of men and elves in the eternal world, but is moved with knowledge of the historical world. In this way, Lúthien's voice unifies the eternal (in her recalling of the creation), historical (by means of her experience, garnered through life in the primary world) and secondary (shown in the song which she creates) worlds together in a more comprehensive way than before. In this respect, her song before Mandos is her greatest.

THE LOSS OF LÚTHIEN: DAERON AND THE NARRATOR

We have seen that the tale of Beren and Lúthien sustains a dialogue on the exact nature of oath and song as subcreative deeds in the historical world, and the impacts and forces behind each. It is implied that song, as a descendent of Eru's creative will, has the power to loose and bind due to the fact that it is creative will which draws back into the historical world memory of the original, unsullied creation. This will enables joy, though all too often the Eagle Effect is hampered in by the effects of oaths broken or exceeded. As the tale of Beren and Lúthien draws to a close there are touches in the text that indicate the narrator's own preoccupation with the loss of Lúthien, and the eucatastrophic ability that she represents.

The narrator of the Beren and Lúthien story is constantly looking to the unification of eternal, history and song, and employs the latter wherever he can, despite his assertion that his tale is without it. In fact, the prose moves in such a way that it very often suggests the eloquence of the song upon which it is based. But the conflict for the narrator is in being caught between the weight of the Beowulfian world in which he writes and the power of song showcased by Lúthien, now lost. It is this collision between the narrator's position and the story he is telling which imbue the tale with so much latent song and a kind of sorrow, even at the moment where Mandos is moved. It is as though the narrator of the Beren and Lúthien story found himself struggling not with the question 'quid Hinieldus cum Christo?'[8], but rather 'what has song to do with man?' It is the same question that Tolkien was answering

---

8. 'What has Ingeld to do with Christ?', Alcuin in a letter to the Bishop of Lindisfarne, AD 797.

when he wrote *Mythopoeia*.

This can be seen in the way the narrator deals with the fate of Daeron, the minstrel who loved Lúthien and later betrayed her love for Beren to Thingol:

> He it was that made music for the dance and song of Lúthien, before Beren came to Doriath; and he had loved her, and set all his thought of her in his music. He became the greatest of all the minstrels of the Elves east of the Sea, named even before Maglor son of Feanor. But seeking for Lúthien in despair he wandered upon strange paths, and passing over the mountains he came into the East of Middle-earth, where for many ages he made lament beside dark waters for Lúthien, daughter of Thingol, most beautiful of all living things. (*TSil*, 216)

At first glance we might put this tale in the same category as Gorlim's dream, a tragic moment representing the weight of the Beowulf syndrome on the text and foreboding the sense of grief that will befall at Lúthien's death. But in this picture of Dearon there are echoes of the narrator of the tale, for it reflects the elegiac note that dominates the text. It is as though the narrator himself laments the loss of Lúthien, and it is this loss which has so powerfully moved his tale. In recounting Lúthien's story the narrator laments her passing from the world, but he has in that lament sought to reach the eternal world which she typified. That nobody 'saw Beren or Lúthien leave the world, nor marked where their bodies lay' (*TSil*, 222) is in many ways a fitting conclusion for the narrative. This ending elevates both Beren and Lúthien to a realm of myth that is in step with the impetus of the eternal world, but which has no reconciliation for their going. The loss of Lúthien is felt by the narrator of *The Silmarillion* throughout the rest of his chronicles, and, more generally, is felt throughout Tolkien's work as the elves as a whole begin to fade.

It is in this way that the grief of *The Silmarillion*'s narrator reflects Tolkien himself. By association with Lúthien the elves become representative in *The Lord of the Rings* of the eucatastrophic and eternal forces that move the world, and their withdrawal to Valinor, much as Lúthien's death, is an elegy for a sense of the eternal missing from our own historical world. Tolkien, a 'singer' bringing forth a whole world in his work, feels the weight of our own world in his writing, and the sorrow at Lúthien's loss is perhaps a reflection of Tolkien's sorrow at the pervading mood of his time.[9]

Lúthien's Legacy: The 'Throbbing String'

Lúthien's loss does not end the connection between song and the eternal: the power of song to denounce and overpower the work of evil and enable life and hope in its stead will be edified again in Sam's song at Cirith Ungol. Here the memory of the story of Beren and Lúthien, figured linguistically in the 'elven stars' (*LotR*, 888) and Sam's assertion that he, unlike Beren in his song of Parting, will not 'bid the stars farewell' (*LotR*, 888), unbinds despair in Sam's historical world when his song is answered. This is one example of many in Tolkien's works, but its scope is to show that eucatastrophe is not tied exclusively to Lúthien, though she represents it strongly. She is a reminder of the ability of song to strike through the dyscatastrophe of the historical world,

---

9. For further discussion, see Anna Thayer, 'Slow-Kindled Courage: A Study of Heroes in the Works of J.R.R. Tolkien', *On Eagles' Wings: An Exploration of Eucatastrophe in Tolkien's Fantasy,* Luna Press Publishing, Edinburgh, 2016, pp. 1-27. First published in *Tolkien and Modernity Vol. II*, in Frank Weinreich and Thomas Honegger, eds, Walking Tree Publishers, Zurich and Berne, 2006, pp. 115-141.

and her last song is a powerful statement of both the value of dyscatastrophe and the power of eucatastrophe. It is the stirring of the unseen 'with a throbbing string'[10], prefigured so powerfully in her song before Mandos, that is Lúthien's legacy to Middle-Earth.

---

10. Op. cit. [2], 'On Fairy Stories', p. 89.

Seeing Fire and Sword, or Refining Hobbits[1]

"My dear Bilbo!" he said. "Something is the matter with you! You are not the hobbit that you were."[2]

Most readers sitting back from Tolkien's tale would nod in sage agreement with Gandalf's diagnosis. For in The Hobbit we see Bilbo Baggins, bumbling everyman from the Shire, stepping into a world peopled by dwarves, wizards, goblins, spiders and, not least, one very large and magnificent dragon. By the final page it would seem fair to say that our hobbit hero has been 'there and back again', and that he has more than amply proven his mettle along the way. We might call it the conventional hero's journey of the conventional everyman hero; but this description would not do justice to Bilbo's adventure, or his character.

This paper will examine Bilbo's role as protagonist, probing what kind of hobbit he has become - or been revealed to be - in a tale that explores and negotiates the boundaries between legends, tales, faërie and ordinary life. By contrasting Bilbo particularly with Thorin, this paper will seek to shed light on Bilbo's pivotal nature as protagonist who both interprets and influences the realm of fire and sword – a trait invariably granted, in Tolkien's works, to hobbits.

> I need a hero. I'm holding out for a hero until the end of the night. He's gotta be strong, he's gotta be fast...

---

[1]. First published 'Der Hobbit' in *Hither Shore Band 5 2008,* DTG, 2008. Also in German in *Tolkiens Grösste Helden: Wie Die Hobbits Die Welt Eroberten,* Bernhard Hennen, ed., Heyne, 2012.

[2]. J.R.R. Tolkien, *The Hobbit*, HarperCollins, London, 1999, first published Allen and Unwin 1937, p. 277. All quotations from *TH* are taken from this edition.

he's gotta be larger than life.[3]

So sings Bonnie Tyler as she holds out for her hero. But is her definition of a hero a kind of 'one-size-fits' all? There are many different types of stories and, unsurprisingly, there are as many different kinds of heroes in them. Like the specimens in a peculiarly literary nature documentary, each hero tends to be well adapted to, or perhaps, the curious product of, the world that he (or she) inhabits.

Most heroes are also in some way beyond the scope of our ordinary world. They are men and women who are accustomed to and refined by experiences of fire and sword. Here are some well-known, predominantly literary, heroes: Achilles; Odysseus; Aeneas; Saint George; Beowulf; Charlemagne; Roland; Lancelot; Hamlet and Bilbo.

Many would agree in classing these men as heroes and also in observing that they are not all heroic in quite the same way. Achilles is the epitome of a classical hero – to use Bonnie Tyler's terms, he is fast, strong and larger than life.

Odysseus' epithet, 'wily', runs before him like fire fanned through dry grass. We have 'pius Aeneas' as the keystone of the new Roman heroism; on the more saintly side we find Saint George and his dragon and, as we can read in dozens of hagiographies, scores of saints who followed similar patterns. Beowulf did better against his monsters than his critics while other heroes, sometimes with the help of those same critics, became literary tropes in their own right. Lancelot, father of the only man who could sit in the siege perilous is, for example, more than partially responsible for both Victorian and mod- ern notions of chivalry. Hamlet,

---

[3]. From 'Holding Out for a Hero', lyrics by Jim Steinman and Dean Pritchford, sung by Bonnie Tyler on her album *Secret Dreams and Forbidden Fire*, first released in 1986 by Columbia Records.

existential thinker caged in a stalling revenge tragedy, has become one of the most famous 'heroes' in literature, aped and marvelled at across the globe.

And Bilbo? It doesn't take critics and academics to note that he is in a completely different league to the other heroes mentioned here. Try imagining him, for example, at the siege of Troy, or facing Grendel's mother in Denmark's swamps, or winding the horn of Roland... It doesn't quite work.

So what kind of hero is Bilbo? Many will answer that he is an everyman, a kind of hero who, perhaps more than any other, is tested by seeing fire and sword. The examination of Bilbo's everyman heroism is the scope of this paper.

Everyman And The Hero's Journey

Our first question has to be: what is an 'everyman'? Enter the *Oxford English Dictionary*, defining an everyman as "an ordinary or typical human being". In fact, the term 'everyman' has been with us a long time, dating back at least as far as mediaeval morality plays. Study of these plays and the OED's definition swiftly leads us to the conclusion that an everyman hero is ordinary or typical, with the purpose of communing with his readers and spectators in a particularly intimate way by means of appealing to common human traits.

We identify keenly with a protagonist who reminds us of ourselves and as we interpret his (or her) experiences through our own eyes, we may even see a trace of ourselves in the unfolding drama. The everyman hero makes the story applicable to us; he both represents us in the story and mediates it to us.

This is, of course, precisely why the everymen are cherished. They differ from the other breeds of heroes – the warriors, thinkers and saints – by being like us: ordinary and typical. Everyman has no supernatural connections, no lost kingdoms, and no murdered fathers. He is the black sheep at the high table of heroes.

Every hero, of course, has a hero's journey, but the everyman's journey is different; he must be pitted against circumstances that are beyond the scope of his experience – and occasionally his understanding – and somehow he must use his wit and noble ordinariness to resolve them. Everyman isn't capable of this at first, and we're used to seeing so-called 'montage' sequences in films where he must be trained, stumbling and failing (usually with a musical accompaniment), before his determination shines through and he succeeds in his task. Once his skills have been finely honed in practice, everyman's journey usually entails demonstrating to the world how the very ordinary can be a mark of greatness in halls peopled by the superhuman.

His task done, everyman returns home happily, enriched in all spheres – but principally in terms of character – by his adventure. Sometimes he even helps to remedy a terrible problem in his society or culture. His story is that of someone unexpectedly called from their normal life to a 'there and back again' adventure. They are, as Shakespeare put it, those who have had "greatness thrust upon them";[4] they are the unexpecting – and sometimes unwilling – subjects for a work of ennoblement in a world beyond their own.

For an example, cast your mind back to the scene at the beginning of Ridley Scott's film *Gladiator*,[5] where the old emperor tells the hero, Maximus, that he wants him to be nominated as emperor after him. Maximus, contrasted against the emperor's own immoral son, has no desire to do so. This is the mirror image to a sentiment expressed in Douglas Adams' *The Hitchhiker's Guide to the Galaxy*, where it is stated that: "Anyone who is capable of getting themselves made President should on no account be

---

4. William Shakespeare, *Twelfth Night*, Act II, Scene V.
5. Ridley Scott, director, *Gladiator*, 2000.

allowed anywhere to do the job".[6]

In Tolkien's own view, the matter of becoming a hero is very similar to that of becoming an emperor. "*Nolo heroizari*" he wrote, "is as good a start for a hero as *nolo episcopari* for a bishop".[7] Saying 'I do not want to be a hero' shows a measure of humility found far too often only in ordinary men. It is that same humility which, at least to the modern eye, forms a fine basis for heroism.

BILBO: 'NOLO HEROIZARI!'

At a first glance Bilbo looks to be the perfect candidate for an everyman hero precisely because he has no desire to be one, and certainly not if it means being the protagonist in an adventure. "'Sorry,' he says to Gandalf, 'I don't want any adventures, thank you. Not today. Good morning! '" (*TH*, 7). Bilbo hides from adventures behind the cloak of his ordinariness. He 'good mornings' Gandalf until he thinks he has 'escaped adventures very well' (*TH*, 8). How many of us have escaped potentially unpleasant – or decidedly unwelcome – situations, in exactly the same fashion?

Tolkien himself sets the frame for us to view Bilbo as the everyman. In a letter to Milton Walden he wrote that *The Hobbit* was "in effect... a study of simple, ordinary man, neither artistic nor noble and heroic".[8] Bilbo's ordinariness is intrinsically borne out in the details and initial representation of his character and in the way his society and culture are figured in the narrator's opening strokes: Bilbo is hedged round by letters, smoke-rings, the Hill

---

6. Douglas Adams, *The Hitchhiker's Guide to the Galaxy: The Original Radio Scripts*, Pan Books Ltd, London, 1985, p. 242.
7. Humphrey Carpenter, ed., *The Letters of J.R.R. Tolkien*, with the assistance of Christopher Tolkien, HarperCollins, London, 1995, first published 1981, p. 215.
8. Op. cit., 'Letters', p. 159.

and the Water, tea and cakes, spare beds and pocket handkerchiefs. From the picture of the pressed and frustrated host trying to be polite to the idly pronounced 'good morning', Bilbo is a well-crafted image of a not quite well-off enough, and comfortingly ordinary, English country gentleman.

But there is a spark in Bilbo that loves tales of the world beyond:

> As [the dwarves] sang the hobbit felt... something Tookish [wake] up inside of him, and he wished to go and see the great mountains, and hear the pine-trees and the waterfalls, and explore the caves, and wear a sword instead of a walking-stick. He looked out of the window. The stars were out in a dark sky above the trees. He thought of the jewels of the dwarves shining in dark caverns. Suddenly in the wood beyond the water a flame leapt up – probably someone lighting a wood fire – and he thought of plundering dragons settling on his quiet Hill and kindling it all to flames. He shuddered; and very quickly he was plain Mr Baggins of Bag-End...again. (*TH*, 16)

This passage is instrumental in illustrating Bilbo as our everyman; the dwarves' song stirs something in him near to a desire for adventure – but the real-world implications of dragons quickly ground him again.

It is about here that our definition of Bilbo as an everyman runs into trouble, for though he may be ordinary Bilbo is not typical in our modern sense. Emphasis is consistently given to the Tookish part of Bilbo and the fact that the dwarves' song moves him at all is further proof of his a-typicality – other hobbits, like Ted Sandyman in *The Lord of the Rings*, would dismiss the kind of song that so affects Bilbo as nonsense.

It seems, therefore, that everyman heroes must be distinguished into at least two groups: the typical everyman, and his ordinary counterpart. Tealess and bumbling around the galaxy in his dressing gown, Arthur Dent from *The Hitchhiker's Guide to the Galaxy* is a fine example of a typical everyman but Bilbo seems to be an ordinary everyman. That is to say, there is something about him that sets him apart from the typical hobbits that surround him, something that is not quite enough to make him extraordinary.

Tolkien commented that "Bilbo was specially selected by the authority and insight of Gandalf as abnormal".[9] Returning to his letter to Walden we find that Tolkien's study of the simple, inartistic man (in this case Bilbo), is actually a study of one who is '*not without the undeveloped seeds of these things*'.[10]

In contrast to the typical everyman the ordinary everyman has the undevel- oped seeds of greater things within him; more than this, perhaps the ordinary everyman is disposed towards making some use of such virtues while a typical everyman is not.

So what ordinary, hidden virtues does Bilbo possess? Tolkien enumerates them in his letters as: "shrewd sense, generosity, patience and fortitude, and also a strong 'spark' yet unkindled".[11] Bilbo has many of these virtues 'blended in good measure' but it is clear that the spark in him is simply waiting to be kindled. The narrator tells us that "Bilbo... got something a bit queer in his make-up from the Took side, something that only waited for a chance to come out" (*TH*, 5).

It is in this part of Bilbo that Gandalf recognises the untapped potential indigenous in his chosen burglar. The hobbit is a perfect subject for the ennoblement that goes with the fire and sword experiences of a hero's journey and we do indeed see ordinary Bilbo from the Shire go from fainting dinner host to dragon-

---

9. Op. cit. [7], 'Letters', p. 365.

10. Op. cit. [7], 'Letters', p. 159, emphasis mine.

11. Op. cit. [7], 'Letters', p. 365.

riddler. Many would comfortable call it the standard fire and sword journey of an everyman. Except for another small problem.

We have seen how, possessing a spark yet unkindled, Bilbo cannot be seen as a typical hobbit – he is an ordinary one. But Bilbo is not simply an ordinary hobbit; he is unexpectedly unconventional, perhaps to the point of disqualifying him from traditional everyman status.

From the outset of the story we are constantly being reminded by the narrator that Bilbo may descend from a line of hobbits who have done exceptional things, like being big enough to ride a horse. And: "it was often said (in other families) that long ago one of the Took ancestors must have taken a fairy wife" (*TH*, 4).

Whether or not Bilbo is disqualified from his everyman status depends very much on our reading of this line. Either it is true that a Took took a fairy wife – meaning that, like more classical heroes, Bilbo has some 'supra-human' ancestry a great distance back – or we must read Tolkien as making an astonishing statement about the nature of being ordinary. In this latter case, it appears that it is perfectly in line for an 'ordinary' hobbit to have a spark that connects him to the fairy world and perhaps this is where the seeds of his undiscovered greatness come from. This unconventional, but apparently ordinary, root further demarks Bilbo from the typical hobbit.

This root engenders a conflict in Bilbo's blood that lends him a veritable verisimilitude: Bilbo both desires and is terrified of adventures, he is entranced and repelled by them. Without this atypical conflict no amount of nudging would have got him to leave his hobbit hole.

This conflict also prepares Bilbo for a much more serious everyman role, that of straddling several worlds. Bilbo has a spark and lives in a commonplace 'familiar' world (being Hobbiton and the Hill). As he is sent running from his hobbit hole by Gandalf he steps into the 'legendary' world of Middle-earth. Just as a good everyman should be, Bilbo is a piece of the ordinary world being driven into the legendary one. And, as he is an ordinary everyman, Bilbo is by no means at ease with the world of wizards, dwarves, goblins and dragons that he goes into.

Bilbo's unease means that he is quick to note discrepancies between the actuality of the legendary world and the depiction of it in the ordinary world from which he came. As they set out the narrator notes that: "Mostly [the weather] had been as good as May can be, even in merry tales, but now it was cold and wet". Bilbo is even less enthused: "'To think it will soon be June,' grumbled Bilbo" (*TH*, 31).

In contrast to Bilbo, the ordinary everyman adjusting to the legendary world, we have a whole company of dwarves and Thorin Oakenshield. The ordinary world of Bilbo's hobbit hole seems, both literally and metaphorically, scarcely enough to hold them. Thorin, dispossessed heir to the King under the Mountain, holds a role comparable in type to that of Aragorn in *The Return of the King*. Yet Thorin is a diminished shadow of the world that he represents. This seems to be caused not by being represented in a tale about a hobbit but by his own nature. Gandalf's description of Thror's exploits in the Necromancer's dungeon sounds as grand and tragic as a heroic exploit should. As the narrator delights in telling us, Thorin's own speech is unnecessarily protracted: "This was Thorin's style... he would probably have gone on like this until he was out of breath, without telling anyone there anything that was not known already" (*TH*, 17). While Gandalf observes repeatedly that there is more to Bilbo than meets the eye, of Thorin, but pages after we have met him, we see Gandalf say that he has been set tasks 'big enough' for him (*TH*, 25).

Set side by side in this fashion we might see Bilbo and Thorin as parallel figures of two descending lines. Bilbo, the ordinary everyman, can either diminish into a quotidian and typical figure by rejecting the call to adventure, or may live to prove the spark in him that does not meet the eye. Thorin, descendant of the legendary world of heroic history, may either become a protracted Lilliputian or a reinstated king.

The stage is set for a tale that explores what it means to be ordinary in the legendary world; it is the very stuff that forges the mettle of the everymen. But the tale isn't just about wringing out the destinies of Bilbo and Thorin by seeing fire and sword, or seeking to reconcile the ordinary and heroic worlds: through Bilbo, Tolkien is also refining the heroism of hobbits and their place in the legendary history of Middle-earth.

LEGENDARY AND COMMONPLACE

Alfred Lord Tennyson once observed that the writing of a good hymn was the most difficult thing in the world for: "In a good hymn you have to be both commonplace and poetical".[12]

Bilbo's story is in many ways like the elusive 'good hymn'; he is caught be- tween the commonplace world and the poetical or legendary one that he knows of primarily through his reading. As soon as he becomes the dwarves' burglar he finds himself pinned between the two. He is no longer seeing fire and sword on the pages of a book – he is living it. Thrust into an adventure beyond his control, Bilbo's occupation of both territories forces him to interpret the dialogue between his own ordinary life and what he meets in the world beyond it.

It is in his interpretation that he becomes an unwitting mediator, both of daily business and sometimes unpleasant legend, to the reader: this mediation and interpretation is the basis of his hero's journey and of his status as an everyman. But it is more than this: the process of interpretation is also the process of his *integration* into the legendary world.

---

12. Hallam Tennyson, *Tennyson: A Memoir*, London, 1899, p. 754.

Initially, Bilbo can only really negotiate the legendary world by relying on Gandalf. It is the wizard who 'interprets' the dwarves' letter, telling Bilbo that he will have to run to be punctual, and frequently it is Gandalf who acts on behalf of Bilbo and the entire company in the various stages of their adventures (such as with the eagles, or in meeting Beorn). A fully integrated part of the world through which they move, the wizard is Bilbo's comfort and encouragement. But as he journeys on Bilbo begins to integrate into the legendary world and as he does so his interpretations of it also become shrewder.

We can exemplify Bilbo's growing (and yet still awkward) integration by looking at his dream in the Misty Mountains: "He dreamed that a crack in the back of the cave got bigger and bigger, and opened wider and wider, and he was very afraid but could not call out or do anything but lie and look. Then he dreamed that the floor of the cave was giving way and he was slipping – begin- ning to fall down, down, goodness knows where to..." (*TH*, 57).

Dreams are very much in the mechanics of fairy and heroic story, and this one is rather prophetic. Bilbo's inability to cry out in the dream is indicative of the fact that he is still only an interpreter or onlooker on the heroic world. In his fear he wakes Gandalf, who will be the key to the dwarves' and hobbit's escape from the goblins. Bilbo's cry, elicited by his dream, affects the waking world – and Gandalf, a key actor in that world – even if it does not grant Bilbo the active ability to do so. It is the first step of an everyman towards not just seeing, but affecting his new surroundings.

The importance of interpretation and its relationship to integrating into and affecting the legendary world is shown keenly in the riddle contest with Gollum. The narrator observes that the finding of the ring, and what follows it, "was a turning point in [Bilbo's] career, but he did not know it" (*TH*, 66). Ironically, it is alone and in the dark that Bilbo begins to recognise the legendary world – he sees that his own blade, glinting dimly in the dark, "is an elvish blade, too" (*TH*, 67). The riddle contest itself has heroic roots; Bilbo knows that "[it] was sacred and of immense antiquity" (*TH*, 76). Like Bilbo, it is a tradition that inhabits both the legendary and commonplace world – many of the riddles exchanged are ones that Bilbo and Gollum know from their time spent living in the latter. Bilbo trades in riddles as simply and deftly as a great hero but does so as an ordinary man. The turning point is in the fact that, alone in the dark, Bilbo has the wit to escape both Gollum and the goblins at the gate. As a prize he retains the ring, itself a tool from the heroic world, and it grants him a legendary aspect when he reappears before the dwarves.

The intertwined nature of the riddling contest is not too far from Bilbo's ordinary experience and yet it is also a heroic and legendary act. Without realising it, Bilbo has come through his first proper deed of fire and sword and gone towards the legendary by interpreting it with the eyes and sense of an ordinary man.

Ordinary Towards Legendary

This is the first of various legendary successes for Bilbo, and his growing integration into the legendary world begins to find expression in heroic tropes: in Mirkwood Bilbo kills the first spider alone and unaided, then names his sword. It makes "a great difference" to him (*TH*, 146). Both killing and naming are steps towards legendary status and yet, just as when Samwise Gamgee battles Shelob, heroism and legends could not be further from Bilbo's mind; his naming of the sword, Sting, seems to come to Bilbo naturally and without any pretensions to heroism.

In this Tolkien gives us both the stereotype and pure type of heroism. We are allowed to appreciate Bilbo's heroism without the blinkers of the heroic canon, even though we are aware of it, and this refreshed appreciation of heroism comes from Bilbo being our everyman.

It can be argued that from this point the narrator's tone keeps us from seeing the full-fledged scale of Bilbo's deeds in Mirkwood. The narrator maintains Bilbo firmly in the guise of an everyman rather than a legendary hero; the details of the time he spends hidden in Thranduil's palace, for example, are kept very much behind the scenes. By means of the ring Bilbo becomes the un-looked-for help in Thorin's despair, using all his cunning to orchestrate the dwarves' escape. It is a testing time of fire and sword in which Bilbo has no help and is, in a sense, more in peril than in his solitary combat with the spiders.

After the great escape the narrator, still showing us the common nature of the protagonist, gives account of Bilbo's cold in reasonable detail. This detail, as well as being one which we would expect from someone who had smuggled himself out of a dungeon in a barrel, seems comic in conjunction with the legendary nature of the escape which Bilbo has effected. With Bilbo's cold it is suddenly the intrusion of the ordinary into the legendary, rather than legendary into the life of the ordinary everyman, that has become the root of the comedy.

This is a key shift in the narrator's tone and demonstrates how far Bilbo's integration has gone. It is relieving to see that our everyman is still 'ordinary', and it is just as well, for it is Bilbo's ordinary everyman nature that saves him from some of the more annoying flaws of traditional and classical heroism: namely, doom and hubris.

Conversing with dragons is, by all accounts, a dangerous business. The narrator tells us as much and we see for ourselves the disturbing and disquieting effect that it has on Bilbo, encouraging him to distrust his friends and allies. Standing before Smaug, however, Bilbo begins to riddle on his names and adventures:

> I am he that walks unseen... I am the clue finder,

> the web-cutter, the stinging fly. I was chosen for the lucky number... I am he that buries his friends alive and drowns them and draws them alive again from the water. I came from the end of a bag, but no bag went over me.... I am the Ring-winner and Barrel-rider... (*TH*, 207)

Bilbo is 'very pleased with his riddling', but if our hero were any kind of hero other than an everyman this would be a moment of terrible hubris. We could compare it, for example, to the consequences of Odysseus giving his name as *nemo* to the Cyclops, or of Turin speaking with Glaurung. If Bilbo was an epic hero, I expect that turning the page would reveal Laketown destroyed by Smaug, the dwarves killed as a consequence of Bilbo's words and Bilbo realising that it had all been his doing before dying in heroic combat against his foe.

But Bilbo is an everyman – he is commonplace, and to Smaug he is out of place: hobbit smell is "quite outside [Smaug's] experience and [puzzles] him mightily" (*TH*, 209). Smaug is confident in his unassailability observing, like Gandalf in the very first chapter, that the like of the heroes of old is "not in the world today" (*TH*, 21, 210). What he fails to recognise is the new kind of hero before him, just as he fails to recognise Bilbo's similarity to his uneasy dream "in which a warrior, altogether insignificant in size but provided with a bitter sword, figured most unpleasantly" (*TH*, 202). Smaug misinterprets his dream because he cannot interpret the ordinary and, in the contest of hobbit and dragon, it is Bilbo's ordinariness that saves him. He extricates himself from his meeting with Smaug with the same platitudes and manner which one might adopt to avoid an awkward dinner with ungainly relatives. It is an everyday skill with which it is likely Bilbo has some experience.

It is Bilbo's unconventional and goading ordinariness that prompts Smaug to go to Laketown where he is slain by Bard. Bilbo's engagement in the heroic trope of speaking with dragons has a good end – except for the dragon – which is as it should be.

Following Smaug's death Thorin is elevated to a legendary status, being at his most eloquent and epic in treating with Bard. But with this elevation he also becomes arrogant. Thorin is not defended from the effect of a dragon hoard and so his reunion with his ancestors' treasure brings him clearly, and negatively, into the legendary heroic canon. On the other hand Bilbo, after various encounters with both dragon and horde, seems to return firmly to his commonplace status.

In the matter of the Arkenstone Bilbo's piercing common sense takes him through the gestures of heroic betrayal in the businesslike guise of an ordinary man doing the best thing that he can think of doing. It is a motive that is not understood by Bard, another representative of the legendary world:

> "...Are you betraying your friends, or are you threatening us?" asked Bard grimly. "My dear Bard!" squeaked Bilbo. "... I am merely trying to avoid trouble for all concerned!" (*TH*, 251)

Bilbo's one true act of burglary – the delivering of the Arkenstone to Bard – is by no means epic. All the same the outcome of the wider adventure rests on it. Even though the theft is little more to Bilbo than an act of common sense, the elves interpret it as a grand gesture:

> The Elvenking looked at Bilbo with a new wonder. "Bilbo Baggins!" he said. "You are more worthy to wear the armour of elf-princes than many who have

looked more comely in it." (*TH*, 251)

Bilbo's ordinariness has metamorphosed before our eyes into a keystone of great- ness. It is just this that Thorin notes when he speaks with Bilbo for the last time: "There is more of good in you than you know, child of the kindly west. Some courage and some wisdom, blended in measure. If more of us valued food and cheer and song above hoarded gold, it would be a merrier world" (*TH*, 266).

By Thorin's death two remarkable things have happened: Bilbo has been re- conciled enough to the legendary world to feel honoured to have shared Thorin's perils, and Thorin sees that there is more to the ordinary world than meets the legendary eye. Through the adventures and interactions of dwarf and hobbit, the ordinary and legendary worlds have been powerfully integrated with each other, to the enrichment of both.

ORDAINED GOODNESS, UNEXPECTED GREATNESS

In his book *The Hero with a Thousand Faces*, Joseph Campbell writes that the hero's journey can begin by means of "a blunder ... the merest chance" which "reveals an unexpected world, and the individual is drawn into a rela- tionship with forces that are not rightly understood. The blunder may amount to the opening of a destiny".[13]

Campbell's definition of a blunder amounting to a destiny might not seem to have a place in the life of an everyman, but it is a key aspect of Bilbo's journey and, through him, a defining and crucial facet of Tolkien's hobbits.

Tolkien wrote that *The Hobbit* was "about the achievements

---

13. Joseph Campbell, *The Hero with a Thousand Faces*, Princeton University, New York, 1949, p. 51.

of ... ordained individuals, inspired and guided by an Emissary to ends beyond their individual education and enlargement".[14]

So Bilbo Baggins, though sharing every nuance of an ordinary everyman, is actually from start to finish to be considered as an ordained everyman, a "chosen burglar" (*TH*, 19). Yet this ordination is beyond the ken of the world in which Bilbo has been ordained to move: the narrator of *The Hobbit* advises us that "no songs alluded... to [Bilbo] even in the obscurest way" (*TH*, 185). Bilbo is both chosen and unforeseen by the conventional wisdoms of either the ordinary or legendary world. As Elrond will later put it in *The Lord of the Rings*: "This is the hour of the Shire-folk, when they arise from their quiet fields, to shake the towers and counsels of the Great. Who of all the Wise could have foreseen it?".[15]

Bilbo's ordinariness has been a platform for the working out of an ordained role. It is the ordinariness that makes our everyman an unlikely candidate; it is beyond the wisdom of the wise.[16] It is this straddling between being elect and being unforeseen, first shown in Bilbo, that refines the hobbits into a race adapted to perform the tasks too great for the heroic races all around them. Bilbo's trial by fire and sword has been a testing ground for the unexpected yet ordained slow-kindled courage that other notable hobbits will exhibit by merit of being ordinary. Hobbits are the distinctly anti-heroic element of Middle-earth and, in this sense, are the ultimate and completely unforeseen channel for the unconventional heroism of the everyman. As heroes, this makes them, in Tolkien's words, "more praiseworthy than the professionals".[17]

---

14. Op. cit. [7], 'Letters', p. 365.

15. J.R.R. Tolkien, *The Lord of the Rings*, HarperCollins, London, 1995, first published in one volume 1968, p. 355.

16. *The Holy Bible New International Version*, Hodder & Stoughton, London, 2000, cf. *1 Corinthians* 1: 20.

17. Op. cit. [7], 'Letters', p. 215.

It is this praiseworthy channelling of unforeseen heroism which gives hob- bits a very literally other-wordly capacity to deliver and reconcile the legendary world into which they travel. The hobbits become agents of eucatastrophe, a means by which a glimpse of *evangelium*, the unlooked for turn, strikes through into Middle-earth. In this, the way in which Tolkien figures the hobbits is partly informed by Tolkien's Christian belief, where an unconventional hero, Christ, by taking an ordinary and human guise eucatastrophically reconciles the historical and eternal worlds.

Hobbits in general – and Bilbo in particular – cannot quite be said to foreshadow Christ, but Bilbo does serve a purpose beyond interpreting and mediating the story to us. In his eucatastrophic journey towards interpretation, integration and reconciliation, Bilbo reminds us to look for the spark in ourselves. We are also everymen – and our ordinary lives are just as capable of being the spring- boards for unexpected heroism, or even ordained eucatastrophe, as a hobbit's. In this sense Bilbo's tale is a call to arms, one that urges us to rise above the typical and ordinary everymen and hear the music of the Lonely Mountain in our hearthside kettle.

'Clean Earth to Till: A Tolkienian Vision of War'[1]

Unlike some fantasy writers, Tolkien was not a man unlessoned in either war or the pity of it. He knew both from first-hand experience and that experience, matched by his faith and love of ancient literature, proved a potent combination when it came to the penning of his works. This paper traces how Tolkien's most famous work envisions war. Particular consideration is given to two distinct types of war – temporal war and a more Ephesians-like spiritual war – and how, in the setting of Middle-earth, particular tenets of literature and faith crucially underpin both. Finally, the paper examines the ends of war – peace and healing – and how, in Tolkien's vision, war and its suffering is made heroic in song and reconciled in clean earth.

INTRODUCTION

It is no secret that a subject as expansive as war is always hard to pin down. Tolstoy was able to write on it at considerable length, and many philosophers and war historians have always done so. This paper is a preliminary investigation into how war is envisioned in one sample of Tolkien's canon of works: accordingly, it cannot and does not pretend to offer a thorough and conclusive investigation into every facet of that vision. Rather, it is an exploration into some aspects of it that seem significant. This exploration will focus on *The Lord of the Rings*, examining the causes, motives, waging and ends of war in the context of the literary and spiritual

---

[1]. First published 'Violence, Conflict and War in Tolkien' in *Hither Shore Band 6 2009,* DTG, 2009.

underpinnings of Tolkien's work. The first question we must ask is what, so far as literary tradition is concerned, are the *causus belli*?
Causus Belli

> Was this the face that launched a thousand ships
> And burnt the topless towers of Ilium?[2]

Many genres of literature intersect over the question of war, handling it differently depending upon the time and function of their writing. One thing is certain: in one form or another, conflict is expected. It drives story-telling. Conflict arises on a sliding scale. It ranges from the microcosmic, focused entirely on inter-personal relations at the level of the individual, and goes through dozens of variations to reach, as is so often the case with the grander end of literature, the macrocosmic, where the focus is on the disputes between nations or worlds. In this latter case of macrocosmic conflict, war and violence by definition almost inevitably play a part in the proceedings. But how do we come to be embroiled in a macrocosmic conflict? This question has troubled philosophers for many years. We can perhaps summarise a very complex process by saying that wars are entered into either to avenge or defend against a perceived or actual wrong, or for gain. The two circumstances can have a considerable measure of overlap.

In the literary genre of fantasy, and especially that sub-genre called heroic fantasy, we will typically encounter a plot where the macrocosmic 'wrong' facing the heroes is that of unlawful dominion. The villain of the piece is either actively seeking or has already obtained a particular gain. Whether he is seizing an inheritance, object of power or entire realm, the heroes' task is either to stop the villain from achieving his ends or to overthrow

---

2. Christopher Marlowe, *Doctor Faustus*, Methuen Educational Ltd, London, 1987, scene xviii, lines 99–100.

him and restore the usurped order. It is the description of the heroes' efforts that make up the story that we read.

It is clear that on a basic level *LotR* uses this kind of plot; all the protagonists' efforts are towards keeping Sauron from seizing unlawful control of Middle-earth. We can see similar traits in other works of modern fantasy: in Narnia, the Pevensys are called upon more than once to drive out usurpers, Prydain's Taran defends against Arawn's increasing power and Earthsea's archmage Ged confronts Cob as he seeks immortality at the cost of the archipelago. Widening our scope a little, Luke Skywalker and his space-faring kindred face exactly the same problems. What unites the heroes of these heroic genres is that they all face villains seeking to destroy or control something that is not theirs to seek. Evil tries to corrupt, pervert and destroy while good tries to redeem, restore and be just.

A villain with his sights set on unlawful dominion is prone to dealing out destruction and violence and doing whatever it takes to obtain his end. Consequentially the stakes in these kinds of stories are often unimaginably high. Failure is measured in suffering and death, and not only for the heroes. This ripple effect means that the heroes' actions take on global or even universal significance. When the final battle-lines are drawn we end up with a rendering of good on one side and evil on the other. Thanks to the macrocosmic nature of this conflict, these lines are not usually metaphorical either – light and dark quite literally go to war.

War in Heaven

The war of good versus evil forms a very particular thread in western story-telling traditions. If we trace it back just three hundred years we find it featuring heavily in Milton's *Paradise Lost*. The concept we encounter is that of war in heaven, good and evil clashing on the grandest scale imaginable. Of course, the meeting of such forces is not unique to the Christian tradition –

but its crucially defining element with that tradition is that good is ultimately and unquestioningly victorious. This is a kind of prevailing wind that quietly breathes life into the genre of heroic fantasy: good triumphs. When it does, virtues other than strength and swords – like hope, charity and courage – often seem to count the most, and the most unlikely and lowly pieces – farmboys, children and peasants – are played against the powers of darkness in the endgame. The biblical parallels are clear: weakness becomes strength, the humble are raised up and the wicked are brought low.

Yet Christianity is not the only tradition wielding power over the fantasy genre. Under our umbrella of the war of good against evil we find a cornucopia of other traditions informing our narratives. They are predominantly pre-Christian and especially, in Tolkien's case, northern. With them come easily-recognisable heroic staples: feats of arms, desperate last stands, battles against impossible odds and deeds done for honour, glory, reputation and song. Over time, these ideas bled into the later, more Christianised notions of mediaeval romances, whose sword-wielding knights were, in their imitation of Christ, also called to moral and spiritual virtue that would have grave consequences in the temporal world.[3] This is the melting pot from which heroic fantasy emerges. The tropes and stances of warfare, whether rooted in sagas and heroic epic or in later Christian ideas of moral and spiritual courage, is a vital ingredient and defining element of the genre.

So, we have the conflict of good and evil and the various virtues and vices of the pagan and Christian traditions. By any culture's definition, righteous or just action is laudable and heroic. Violence and war must be faced with physical skill and spiritual strength. Sometimes, as in the case of Spenser's knight Guyon throwing down the 'bowres of blisse' in *The Faerie Queene*, physical deeds

---

3. In terms of the relations between virtue and physical action, *Sir Gawain and the Green Knight* is a highly articulated case in point.

are morally and spiritually motivated. The rule seems simple: fight the good fight, and all will be well.

But life in a work of modern heroic fantasy is more complicated than this. For writers of Tolkien's generation, and in many cases those writing after him even up to our own day, we also have to add to this mix the issues thrown up by a world disenchanted with morality, heroism and above all with war. Fantasy lives still in the literary shadow of the Great War and many writers, especially in Tolkien's time, swallowed that era's aversion to war and its relentless questioning of whether bloodshed and sacrifice can ever be justified, or achieve the good, whatever that might be. In other words, can war ever be good, whether it is thought of as a 'just war' or not?

Tolkien's works are born in these complex literary circumstances, just as Tolkien's writing is itself born in times of war and nurtured by 'the desire to express [his] feelings about good, evil, fair [and] foul'.[4] Perhaps because of the press of disillusionment in his contemporaries and his own encounters with violence, Tolkien found himself driven to talk about good, evil and war. The emerging fantasy genre, a product of the classics and sagas and Christian thought, was his chosen vehicle. Tolkien powerfully reconnected heroic fantasy to its literary and warfaring roots, creating a vision of war that stood against the status quo of his time. He does this by re-establishing war's morality in terms of its temporal and spiritual ends. Tolkien builds up a picture of a just war, but never denies the very human complexity of being in the line of battle.

---

4. Humphrey Carpenter, ed., *The Letters of J. R. R. Tolkien*, with the assistance of Christopher Tolkien, HarperCollins, London, 1995, Letter 66, p. 78.

Spectrums of Response

In *LotR* Tolkien presents us with the vast canvas of a world at war where each culture and character responds differently to the threat posed by the Dark Lord. In fact, just as some critics have called Tolkien's most famous work a travelogue we might also call it an opinion poll, one whose results show attitudes to war that would be at home among cultures far earlier than ours, as well as our own. Everyone that we meet on the road to Mordor has a slightly different take on the war that will end the Third Age. There are those who help and those who hinder, those who are passionate and those who are indifferent, those who stridently face the situation with all their courage and those who will not look it in the eye. Tolkien presents us with a spectrum of responses – some of them canonically heroic, some of them decidedly post-modern, and all of them very human. Most characters can be read as a confluence of the literary and historical tradition they represent and that tradition's stance on virtue and on war. Tolkien uses these points of confluence as a way of exploring and re-envisioning a just war.

An excellent example of this kind of exploratory confluence is in the Rohirrim and, more specifically, in Théoden. Rohan is a culture that seems at once Anglo-Saxon, Norse and Classical: it has a sense of northern spirit in its literary links to the tale of *Beowulf* and in its emphasis on deeds and song. This same emphasis also links the Rohirrim to the heroes of ancient Greece, whose deeds sought glory, *kleos*, while in nomenclature Théoden's people are clearly linked to the Anglo-Saxons. Tolkien presents us with a people whose concerns seem to be centred on war:

> Where now the horse and the rider? Where is the horn that was blowing?
> Where is the helm and the hauberk, and the bright

hair flowing?
Where is the hand on the harpstring, and the red fire glowing?[5]

This elegiac verse by 'a forgotten poet' is clearly indebted to the Anglo-Saxon alliterative tradition. It shows us that song-making for the Rohirrim, as for many historical peoples, is commemorative, and demonstrates that a driving purpose for these songs is to remember war, and those lost in it. The song for the horse and the rider connects war ('the helm and the hauberk'), beauty ('the bright hair flowing'), song ('the hand on the harpstring') and the singing of songs by the fire ('the red fire glowing') together. By doing so, Tolkien suggests that song and war encompass every aspect of the Rohirrim's existence, from the cradle to the grave. Peter Jackson took up this idea in his film version: in the extended edition of *The Two Towers* we see Éowyn singing a funerary dirge for Théodred:

> Bealocwealm hafað fréone frecan forth
> onsended giedd sculon singan gléomenn sorgiende
> on Meduselde.
>
> [An evil death has set forth the noble warrior / A song shall sing sorrowing minstrels in Meduseld.] [6]

The fact that the death was evil and the warrior noble compounds our sense that the warrior's participation in war was a just one. At the same time, the minstrel's lament guarantees that

---

5. J.R.R. Tolkien, *The Lord of the Rings*, HarperCollins, London, 1995, p. 497. All quotations from *LotR* are taken from this edition.

6. Quote and translation from <http://www.warofthering.net/forum/vbulletin225/upload/showthread.php?t=5852> [accessed 1 August 2012].

this noble warrior will be remembered.

When Théoden is contemplating the final defence of the Hornburg Tolkien again sketches for us how outstanding deeds of martial heroism – and remembering them in song – is of crucial concern to the Rohirrim:

> When dawn comes, I will bid men sound Helm's horn, and I will ride forth. Will you ride with me then, son of Arathorn? Maybe we shall cleave a road, or make such an end as will be worth a song – if any be left to sing of us hereafter. (*LotR*, 527)

Théoden uses the vocabulary of epic: Aragorn is the epithetical 'son of Arathorn', the killing is presented in terms of cleaving – a vivid verb suggesting mass bloodshed – and the deed is to be worth a song. Théoden's connecting of song, memory and noble deeds done in war is a rendering of an ethos familiar to us from both Classical and Northern sources – a cursory glance through the pages of *Beowulf* or Homer's *Iliad* would furnish us with many examples for comparison. These ideas add up to show us that, for the Rohirrim, the battlefield is a place where virtue is proven by noble, violent deeds and songs are written to perpetuate that nobility.

With epic language and gestures left, right and centre, we seem to be dealing with a culture that exclusively values martial and physical prowess. However, Tolkien adds another layer of depth to the Rohirrim when King Théoden parts with Wormtongue:

> "Give him a horse and let him go at once, wherever he chooses," said Gandalf. "By his choice you shall judge him."
>
> "Do you hear this, Wormtongue?" said Théoden. "This is your choice: to ride with me to war, and let

us see in battle whether you are true; or to go now, whither you will. But then, if we ever meet again, I shall not be merciful." (*LotR*, 509)

It is subtle, but in this short quotation we see moral notions of judgement, mercy, and forgiveness underscoring warring acts – and all are crucially tied to the element of choice. Théoden makes it clear that battle is a place where a man can prove true in his fealty, but he also implicitly agrees with Gandalf that Wormtongue's choice is the keenest measure of his truth. It is implied that achievement in battle is only worthy if it is 'true', and that truth can only be judged by a man's choices. The heroism of choice is a much more Christian idea – one that is crucial to Frodo's non-violent protagonism – and Tolkien here suggests that the moral and spiritual capacity to be true and choose rightly must be the precursor to any deed in battle. This concept of what we might call *jus in delectu* – not just in war but just in choice – is crucial to Tolkien's view of the relations between morality, deeds and war.

The aligning of morality with martial skill is a step towards the world of mediaeval romance, and a firm step away from our first impressions of Théoden's hall as a place of song and glory, firmly in the tradition of Hrothgar's own. Despite the best efforts of Augustine, St. Thomas Aquinas, and the company of just war theory, uniting morality and war under one banner can seem contradictory, and doubly so to those enchanted by blind pacifism. Indeed, once Théoden arrives at Isengard, Saruman is quick to try to work the apparent incongruity of the epic stance and moral choice against our heroes:

"Am I to be called a murderer, because valiant men have fallen in battle? If you go to war, needlessly, for I did not desire it, then men will be slain. But if I am

> a murderer on that account, then all the House of Eorl is stained with murder; for they have fought many wars, and assailed many who defied them." (*LotR*, 566)

Saruman uses heroic language ('valiant men', 'slain') to cast moral aspersions on Théoden, implying that war and morality are incompatible. Morality affects the semantics of war: if he wishes to be moral Théoden will have to reinterpret all the heroic deeds that the Rohirrim hold so dear as nothing more than murder. In other words, Saruman insists that morality must equate with inaction and pacifism. The Rohirrim are not pacifists and therefore cannot be moral. Saruman's intent is to divorce warfare from its moral and heroic roots.

This conversation with Saruman represents a different kind of conflict for Théoden – this is not a battle against 'flesh and blood' but against the convincing power and authority of Saruman's voice. It is an 'inner war',[7] and it is Théoden's growing moral courage that enables him to withstand the onslaught:

> "We will have peace," he said, *now in a clear voice*, "we will have peace, when you and all your works have perished – and the works of your dark master to whom you would deliver us." (*LotR*, 566, emphasis mine)

Théoden's language here is uncompromising and may even seem extreme, yet it is unquestioningly the right answer. Théoden has become a channel for a steely glimmer of the heroism of moral choice, epitomised throughout *LotR* by Frodo. The biblical – and in every way apocalyptic – resonance of his words takes us back to

---

7. Op. cit. [4], Letter 71, p. 82.

the idea of a battle of light against dark, one that is conducted both in a temporal and spiritual plane. It also gives us a bold picture of the ultimate goal of war – peace, as defined by the perishing of all the works of evil. That Théoden's voice here is 'clear' is a signal to the reader that he is doing rightly and that, in line with Pauline tradition,[8] Tolkien views moral and spiritual capacity as vital and as necessary in war as feats of arms. War is waged in the material and the spiritual worlds, but on both planes it must be waged with *clarity*.

We have seen the Rohirrim move from the ranks of the classical and northern traditions towards the mediaeval allegorical stance of the inner war, where morality and physical courage must have a symbiotic relationship. We have also seen how Tolkien uses this progression to highlight the compatibility of spirituality, morality and arms – a mixture that would have seemed out of place to a generation still reeling from Paschendale and the Somme. Having taken, in Théoden's encounter with Saruman, a step towards the apocalyptic, Tolkien also ideologically here sets the scene for the Rohirrim at the battle of the Pelennor where, driven forward by a moral conviction in the justice of joining battle:

> They sang as they slew, for the joy of battle was on them and the sound of their singing that was fair and terrible came even to the city. (*LotR*, 820)

The admixture of singing that is 'fair and terrible' with battle creates the flavour of an apocalyptic vision: the representation has something in common with passages in the book of Revelations. Tolkien presents a brief and stunning prefiguring of the war in heaven whose eschatological nature heightens our perception of

---

8. See for example, 'Ephesians', *The Holy Bible*, New International Version.

the necessity of the moral strength needed to face evil. It also acknowledges the inherent contradiction at the heart of war – it is both fair and terrible.

Tolkien compounds his argument for the necessity of moral conviction by presenting Denethor as a foil to Théoden. While Théoden has clarity Denethor has become clouded by despair:

> "Pride and despair!" he cried ... "thy hope is but ignorance. Go then and labour in healing! Go forth and fight! Vanity!... The West has failed ... I will have naught: neither life diminished, nor love halved, nor honour abated." (*LotR*, 835–56)

Denethor's moral sin of despair withdraws him from battle and compels him into taking his own life – an act only previously performed by 'heathen kings, under the domination of the Dark Power'.[9] Tolkien uses Denethor to underline the necessity of choosing hope and taking a stand in war, showing his belief that '...it has [been,] is and will be necessary to face [war] in an evil world'.[10] In his letters Tolkien writes of the material, moral and spiritual 'waste' of war – of which Denethor, in his lack of stewardship, moral discernment, and overarching despair, seems emblematic. This same despair pejoratively labels both fighting and healing as 'vanity' – and, paradoxically, Tolkien's use of Denethor here brings healing to the reader's attention as one of the ends of war.

Denethor is not alone in grappling with despair; another character hounded by it is Éowyn:

---

9. It is interesting to note that the word *heathen* is one of the few religiously charged words to remain in the text following Tolkien's careful removal of them. This heightens the notion that despair is a moral sin.
10. Op. cit. [4], Letter 63, p. 75.

> [Merry] caught the glint of clear grey eyes; and then he shivered, for it came suddenly to him that it was the face of one without hope who goes seeking death. (*LotR*, 785)

This use of 'clear' is very different to when we saw it used to describe Théoden's moral clarity. Tolkien is not suggesting that Éowyn's desire to seek death is morally correct or glorious. Rather, by juxtaposing the apparent clearness of her eyes with their colour, 'grey', he suggests the clouding of her internal, moral clarity by despair. While going to battle may be an outward gesture of nobility and courage the signal to the reader (compounded by Merry's shivering) is that there is no moral virtue behind this gesture. Tolkien shows that despair can look very much like heroism from the outside, but that heroism without internal moral decisiveness is 'without hope'. I have little doubt that Tolkien had seen its like in fellow soldiers in the trenches.

You may be thinking that this use of the virtues of hope and the vices of despair as a way of defining a character's moral capacity is a clean-cut system inside a work of fantasy: hope = good = just in war, despair = bad = violent in war. But we all know that the real world is more complicated than this. Like Samwise on the road to Mordor, we are afflicted by hope and despair in turns, and have likely all felt how it affects our judgements. Tolkien has often been charged with 'escapism', and perhaps a superficial and simplistic view of Tolkien's dialogue of hope and despair has contributed to that charge. Although he is showing us a moral system Tolkien is not giving us a 'disneyfied' vision of hope and despair. On the contrary, he makes the very human recognition that at the toughest moments in our lives – at the end of all things or at the very brink – 'hope and despair are akin' (*LotR*, 862), when Imrahil asks:

> "... you would have us retreat to Minas Tirith ... and

there sit like children on sand-castles when the tide is flowing?' said Imrahil.

"That would be no new counsel," said Gandalf. "Have you not done this and little more in all the days of Denethor? But no! I said this would be prudent. I do not counsel prudence. I said victory could not be achieved by arms. I still hope for victory, but not by arms." (*LotR*, 860)

The dialogue between hope and despair as moral forces for driving temporal warfaring action is made very clear during the last debate. In fact, the Aristotelian sense of the word 'prudent' here alerts us, as readers, to the tricky mid-way between hope and despair that the heroes are attempting to fare. The decision to march out and make a last stand is canonically and classically heroic, while the determination to do so self-sacrificially for Frodo, thus leaving his heroism of choice and pity the hoped-for time to triumph, has definite moral connotations. The march is neither entirely altruistic nor entirely desperate. If we weigh it we find that Aragorn's decision defies canonisation – it is too altruistic to sit in the heroic camp and too desperate to sit in the moral one. In this regards it is the denouement to Tolkien's vision of war. War is not glorified. Tolkien recognises that the real, historic world, unlike the world of sub-creation, cannot simply be divided into canons of northern or moral heroism or into camps of light and dark, good and evil. As Tolkien put it in his letters: 'In real (exterior) life men are on both sides: which means a motley alliance of orcs, beasts, demons, plain naturally honest men, and angels'.[11] While acknowledging this historical grey-scale in the morality of men, Tolkien's portrayal of his heroes suggests that the 'naturally honest men and angels' are those who inform their

---

11. Op. cit. [4], Letter 71, p. 82.

deeds with moral clarity – and that, if waged with moral clarity, war can be just and good.

THE END OF ALL THINGS AND THE ENDS OF WAR

At this point we must ask: what are the ends of war? The canvas of a battle of light against dark, and the associated underpinning of both spiritual and temporal war, could lead us to the conclusion that, for Tolkien, the end of war is in apocalypse – if our heroes are driven to act morally and righteously against evil villains then war must lead to the final showdown between good and evil. While this is an understandable conclusion to draw it isn't a whole one. Although, dramatically speaking, the story ends with the destruction of the Ring and the crowning of Aragorn that is not where Tolkien chooses to end his narrative. To those who complain of the 'multiple endings' of *LotR* this can seem incomprehensible. Why doesn't Tolkien stop at what seems to be the natural end of his tale – where the fighting finishes?

This refusal to end the story with the end of the fighting points to a much deeper vision of war. For the first traces of our answer we must look back to the despair of Denethor. Tolkien unveils that despair as moral corruption and underscores that message by showing us how even in his despair, Denethor paradoxically thinks of healing. Although the Steward dismisses healing as an unthinking travail he is still aware that it is the compassed goal of those who desire to keep on fighting. And when Éowyn, another victim of despair, comes to understand her heart her new-found clarity shows her that she 'will be a shieldmaiden no longer, nor vie with the great Riders, nor take joy only in the songs of slaying. [She] will be a healer, and love all things that grow and are not barren' (*LotR*, 943). There are, as Tolkien put it in his letters, those who are needed for 'things other than war'.

As *LotR* winds to its conclusion peace, as defined by healing, sowing and rebirth and the turning of swords into ploughshares, is shown as the end of war – but Tolkien does not hand us peace on a silver platter. It is a process, as the ever practical Samwise Gamgee observes, of 'clear[ing] up the mess' which takes 'a lot of time and work' (*LotR*, 997). Unlike many writers of the genre, Tolkien invests time and effort into considering the after-effects of war – and he does not sugar-coat it. Sometimes, what seem to us as the best possible legacy of moral choices doesn't quite work out.

After the scouring of the Shire Frodo – who, in being 'wounded by knife, sting, tooth and a long burden' is both temporally and spiritually injured – 'drop[s] quietly out of all the doings of the Shire'. The Shire has been saved, 'but not for [him]' (*LotR*, 1002). Tolkien acknowledges that an inevitable consequence of war is that not all 'victors [are] able to enjoy victory'.[12] This is something he would not have been able to show had the story ended at Mount Doom. Haunted by darkness and the lingering horror that he did not give up his life to destroy the Ring,[13] Frodo withdraws from his active narrative role, encouraging Sam to take it in his place:

> The title page had many titles on it, crossed out one after another.
> "Why, you have nearly finished it, Mr. Frodo!" Sam exclaimed …
> "I have quite finished, Sam," said Frodo. "The last pages are for you." (*LotR*, 1004)

In his depiction of Frodo's consuming hurt, Tolkien shows us that those who are too deeply tainted by war long after the 'hidden

---

12. Op. cit. [4], Letter 181, p. 235.
13. In some ways, this could be seen as a Christianised or 'martyrish' version of classical *kleos*.

paths' that lead to 'a far green country under a swift sunrise'. The spiritual heroism that sustained Frodo to the Crack of Doom has been exhausted. Frodo is juxtaposed with Sam, who takes an active role in healing the Shire and whom Frodo calls his 'heir'. By presenting Sam as an heir to 'everything [Frodo] had and might have had' (*LotR*, 1006), Tolkien is also making Sam the heir to Frodo's moral heroism of choice. It is something Sam must use when deciding what to do with his gift from Galadriel:

> "I'm not sure the Lady would like me to keep it all for my own garden, now so many folk have suffered," said Sam.
> "Use all the wits and knowledge you have of your own, Sam," said Frodo, "and then use the gift to help your work and better it …"
> So Sam planted saplings in all the places where specially beautiful or beloved trees had been destroyed … and at the end he found that he still had a little of the dust left; so he went to the Three-Farthing Stone, which is as near the centre of the Shire as no matter, and cast it in the air with his blessing. (*LotR*, 1000)

Initially under Frodo's tutelage and then independently, Sam comes to embody how the moral heroism of choice so necessary in war is to be turned into a force of rejuvenation once violence is ended. Tolkien's description of the following summer seems to compound the spiritual virtue of Sam's choice: 'Not only was there wonderful sunshine and delicious rain, in due times and perfect measure, but there seemed something more: an air of richness and growth, and a gleam of a beauty beyond that of mortal summers that flicker and pass upon this Middle-earth' (*LotR*, 'The Grey Havens' 1000). The heroism that led in times of war to the destruction of the Ring leads, in times of peace, to clean fields and

The Fields That We Know

We have seen how Tolkien's vision is clearly conscious of the temporal and spiritual aspects of war, and the necessity of acting from a clear moral standpoint. This vision of war in the sub-created world enables the division of good from evil, hope from despair and morality from indifference, attributes that contribute to an apocalyptic feel but which serve to highlight the virtue and necessity of moral, spiritual and temporal good. Ultimately, *LotR* recognises war as something to be faced with courage and faith for, as Tolkien writes in his letters: 'evil labours with vast power and perpetual success – in vain: preparing always only the soil for unexpected good to sprout in'.[14] This is a vision that recognises the final haven of humanity from war in a place where there shall be 'no more weeping', and sees that our earth-bound lives are caught in a struggle against evil. Throughout his work and especially his letters, Tolkien acknowledges that in our temporal plane we will always be called upon to go to war, whether literally or metaphorically. Evil will happen, but each of us has a moral and spiritual obligation to stand against it where we find it, and to pursue peace:

> "Other evils there are that may come … yet it is not our part to master all the tides of the world, but to do what is in us for the succour of those years wherein we are set, uprooting the evil in the fields that we know, so that those who live after us may have clean earth to till. What weather they shall have is not ours

---

14. Op. cit. [4], Letter 64, p. 76.

to rule". (*LotR*, 861)

These fields, cleaned by clear-hearted moral heroism, are the ultimate end of war – and they are to be worked no less courageously in times of peace.

Stars Above a Dark Tor: Tolkien and Romanticism[1]

A profound shift in the West's attitudes to art and human creativity, Romanticism's focus was on freedom of self-expression: this found its culmination in the exultation of the spontaneity and originality of the individual imagination. This imagination was to break through the status quo of contemporary literature, turning the Romantic pen back towards myth and legend, the transcendent qualities of nature and a renewed relationship with language. Whether celebrating the sublime ardour of the poet's creative imagination, indulging in the excesses of sensitivity or unleashing the new stirrings of the Gothic, the Romantics were a force of renewal in literature. Tolkien found himself working with the literary legacy of the Romantics. This paper will overview Romanticism in general terms and, with specific reference to The Lord of the Rings, assess in what ways Tolkien's writings can be considered to be the work of a Romantic author. This examination will, in turn, allow a more detailed consideration of how Tolkien both uses and reworks the Romantic impulse.

'The beauty of it smote his heart... and hope returned to him.'[2]

Imagine an English Romantic poet. What kind of picture comes to mind? Perhaps an indolent young man, quill in hand, ambling through the countryside? Or something much wilder – a visionary poet with wind-driven hair?

---

1. First published 'Tolkien and Romanticism' in *Hither Shore Band 7 2010,* DTG, 2010.
2. J.R.R. Tolkien, *The Lord of the Rings*, HarperCollins, London, 1995, p. 957. All quotations from *LotR* are taken from this edition.

Out of barbaric curiosity, I tested this same question on some of my students. Their responses ranged from 'Some wet guy with flowing hair, moping in a field writing' to just two words: 'Oh God!' The latter student was not enamoured with English and its great literary heritage (and ambushing them in the lunch queue probably didn't help).

What my students' answers do suggest is that the Romantics are commonly misunderstood; the passing of two centuries sometimes blinds us to what is most fundamental about them.

The Romantics were radicals, thinking and writing about as far outside the contemporary box as it was possible for poets and writers in their time to go. Anti-establishmentarianism could have been their middle name. In every sphere – philosophical, ideological, political, religious and literary – these 18th century bad boys represented a threat to the establishment. These were the kind of men that sweet old ladies would shake their heads at. Worse than bad and ugly – they were considered mad and dangerous to know.

Why? The Romantic movement created a profound shift in the West's attitudes to art and human creativity. Classical purity was formal and stiff-necked, and stifling neo-classical imitation seemed to repress the glory of the human spirit. This was not, to use a delightful English idiom, the Romantics' 'cup of tea'. Going entirely against the grain of contemporary literary thought, they turned inwards to unleash their innermost capacities of self-expression, exulting in the spontaneity and originality of their individual imaginations.

It was a Promethean exploit. In fact, we might take the story of Prometheus as a good symbol for what the Romantics were trying to achieve – they were wresting back the fire of the human spirit – imagination – for the use of all mankind. Unlike its classical counterpart, however, this Romantic Prometheus is released – just as he is in Shelley's closet drama *Prometheus Unbound*.

Imagination is the presiding spirit of the Romantic movement. It was the visionary capacity that allowed the Romantic pen to strike back to a realm of myth and legend so as to capture the transcendence of nature and sheer presentness of human existence. More even than presiding spirit, imagination was the Romantics' very lifeblood, and it ran throughout Europe.

THE WILD, THE IMPROBABLE, THE FANCIFUL: ENGLAND'S ROMANTICS

Asked to name the six key figures of English Romanticism, any good student of English Literature will list William Blake, William Wordsworth, Samuel Taylor Coleridge, John Keats, Percy Bysshe Shelley and Lord Byron as the guilty parties. These poets range from the truly visionary to the revolutionary and the outright tragic. They were all prolific writers - any one of them might claim Ozymandias' infamous words: 'look on my works, ye mighty, and despair'. Tigers, albatrosses, daffodils and Grecian urns had perhaps never before enjoyed such notoriety as these poets gave them. And, although they may have differed in opinion on some details, the heart of their theories of poetry was the same: everything resided in the crucial role of the imagination.

William Blake perhaps put it most clearly when he wrote: 'This world of imagination is the world of eternity'.[3] Indeed, for Coleridge, imagination was 'the living Power and prime Agent of all human Perception... a repetition in the finite mind of the eternal act of creation in the infinite I AM'.[4] More personably than his co-Romantics, Keats wrote: 'I am certain of nothing but the holiness of the heart's affections and the truth of the imagination'.[5]

---

3. William Blake, *Poetry and Prose of William Blake*, ed. Geoffrey Keynes, Nonesuch Press, London, 1939, p. 639.
4. S.T. Coleridge, *Biographia Literaria*, vol. 1, ed. J. Shawcross, Clarendon Press, Oxford, 1907, p. 202.
5. Quotation from Keats' letter to Benjamin Bailey, 22 November

This is what we might, with hindsight, call a eucatastrophic vision of literature. However it is expressed the essential sentiment is the same: there is something about imagination that transcends human experience and puts it back in touch with higher, eternal truths. The city of London, reviled by Blake as a place where 'soldiers' sighs/ Run in blood down palace walls'[6] is mystically redeemed in its reconnection to the glories of creation when Wordsworth finds its smokeless morning sleep as much a thing of splendour as the Edenic first light on valley, rock and hill.

This is linguistically and ideologically powerful stuff. But the Romantic imagination entailed far more than lounging about on London bridges writing sonnets. This notion of imagination was all-encompassing. For the Romantics, imagination meant breaking away from the classical unities of form and structure; spurning the trappings of rationalism in favour of the feeling of individual experience; and rejecting the rapidly expanding grind of urban life so as to return to man's true setting – nature, free from the 'mind-forged manacles' of a mechanistic view of life. It was an ideal vision of the world in so far as it was rooted entirely in ideas.

Needless to say, the Romantics were not very high up on Locke and Newton's Christmas card lists. Romanticism was an 'all or nothing' affair. You could not be half-hearted in this line of literature.

Transposing these ideals of imagination from mind to paper might seem a daunting prospect. But these poets were nonplussed by the challenge. They saw themselves as inheritors of the great romances, those 'wild, improbable... fanciful' tales that were 'full of wild scenery'.[7] Imagination was the key – and these writers

---

1817, <http://www.john-keats. com/briefe/221117.htm> [accessed 12 November 2015].

6. William Blake, *William Blake: Songs of Innocence and of Experience*, ed. Richard Wilmott, Oxford University Press, Oxford, 2001, p. 38.

7. S.T. Coleridge, *Letters of Samuel Taylor Coleridge*, vol. 1, ed. Ernest

used it to unlock new styles and types of literature.

IMAGINATION: THE DIVINE VISION

It is by now clear that in order to grasp the Romantics we need to grapple with the idea of imagination. The OED defines it, rather dryly, as 'the faculty or action of forming ideas or mental images'. Imagination is a concept that, from our earliest childhoods, is set in stern opposition to reality. Tolkien himself acknowledges this in *On Fairy Stories*, where he explores how fantastical literature can be condemned as escapist and juvenile. This trend goes back at least as far as Plato's theory of forms – imagination here is considered as a step too far from the true nature of things, leading to the expulsion of poets from the Republic. Even today, imagination is seemingly divorced from any redemptive creative wellspring – its places are the nursery or the business board room. Phrases like 'he has an over-active imagination' or 'you're just imagining things' point to a certain distrust of this human faculty.

For Blake, imagination was 'the divine vision', one that enabled you to see 'a world in a grain of sand'.[8] Tolkien would go on to make this same connection, both in *Mythopoeia* (where he writes to C. S. Lewis that 'we make still by the law in which we're made')[9] and *On Fairy Stories*. For Tolkien, as for the Romantics, the process of subcreation – a divinely ordained imagining of other worlds – is not only innately but vitally human, connecting us to creation itself in a way that few other processes are capable of doing.

In many ways, we can view Tolkien's minor work *Leaf by*

Hartley Coleridge, Houghton Mifflin, Boston and New York, 1895, p. 352.

8. Op. cit. [3], Blake, p. 11.

9. J.R.R. Tolkien, 'Mythopoeia' in *Tree and Leaf*, HarperCollins, London, 2001, first published Allen and Unwin 1964, p. 87.

Niggle as a deeply personal and thinly-veiled allegorical dialectic exploring this very issue. Niggle spends as much of his life as he can working on his painting of a tree, but it is only after he leaves the purgatorial Workhouse and goes on to Niggle's Country that the truer nature of his painting is revealed:

> A great green shadow came between him and the sun. Niggle looked up and fell off his bicycle.
> Before him stood *the* Tree, his Tree, finished. If you could say that of a tree that was alive, its leaves opening, its branches growing and bending in the wind that Niggle had so often felt or guessed, and so often failed to catch. He gazed at the Tree, and slowly lifted his arms and opened them wide.
> 'It's a gift!' he said. He was referring to his art, and also to the result; but he was using the word quite literally.[10]

Tolkien clearly aligns himself here with what we might call a Romantic mode of imagination. If we take Niggle's tree as an allegorical expression of the role of imagination in art, then it is a gift, to be used wisely (as the rest of Niggle's tale clearly shows). But the tree is only truly finished once its mimetic quality – the way in which its artistry mirrors something definitive and eternal – is revealed. The art brings us a step closer to the high, eternal form. In this way, Tolkien's view of imagination assimilates and inverts Plato's theory of forms:

> 'Niggle's Picture!' said Parish in astonishment. 'Did

---

10. J.R.R. Tolkien, *Tales from the Perilous Realm*, HarperCollins, London, 2009, p. 299 (emphasis mine). All quotations from *LN* are taken from this edition.

you think of all this, Niggle? I never knew you were so clever. Why didn't you tell me?'

'He tried to tell you, long ago,' said the man, 'but you would not look. He had only got canvas and paint in those days, and you wanted to mend your roof with them. This is what you and your wife used to call Niggle's Nonsense...'

'But it did not look like this then, not real,' said Parish.

'No, it was only a glimpse then,' said the man; 'but you might have caught the glimpse, if you had ever thought it worth while to try.' (*LN*, 141)

As for the Romantics, imagination is a gift, a divine vision, a subcreative act that can reconnect man to the divine. Rather than removing us from the true nature of things Tolkien argues that it can offer us a heart-shattering glimpse of them. It was an idea that would find academic crystallisation in his concept of eucatastrophe. Pursuing the creative impulse grants us a glimpse of eternity – in Niggle's case, 'an introduction to the Mountains'. C. S. Lewis called the same 'glimpsing' experience 'Joy'. Blake, with his accustomed visionary vigour, likens that moment of transcendent clarity to 'Hold[ing] infinity in the palm of your hand / and eternity in an hour.'[11]

PAINTING NIGGLE'S TREE: IMAGINATION IN ACTION

Imagination is the envisioning of something beyond reality, something which perhaps offers a glimpse of eternity. So far so good – but how do you get a transcendent experience neatly down onto an obliging bit of paper?

---

11. Op. cit. [3], Blake, p. 118.

The Romantics almost invariably turned to poetry. The choice is an obvious one – it could be argued that few other literary forms offer the writer such an intense vehicle of expression, replete as it is with the subtleties of rhythm, diction and imagery. Poetry is an ancient and aural art, one that forces the listener or reader to open their own imagination to the writer's vocalised vision. Take, for example, the hypnotic power of William Blake's *The Tiger* – a poem which is itself concerned with subcreation:

> Tiger, Tiger, burning bright
> In the forests of the night:
> What immortal hand or eye
> Could frame thy fearful symmetry? [...]
>
> When the stars threw down their spears,
> And watered Heaven with their tears,
> Did he smile his work to see?
> Did he who made the lamb make thee? [...][12]

The tight rhymes and relentless rhythm of Blake's poem convey a sense of awe and urgency in a way that perhaps no prose can. This visionary lyric assaults the senses, forcing an imaginative response in its arresting language and questioning of the reader – we cannot evade it. Blake's choice of poetic form and structure are exact.

Of course, Tolkien's works are not renowned for their poetry – although one can (and I would!) argue for the astonishing, eucatastrophic power of Sam's song in Cirith Ungol or the almost unbearable poignancy of *Bilbo's Last Song*. But that is not to say that we must bar Tolkien from his Romantic heritage on account of his choice of form; we often have a special reverence for poetry,

---

12. Op. cit. [6], Songs, p. 34.

tending to view it as the highest form of literary expression. At times that is well deserved. But we should not forget that our word poetry derives, after all, from the Greek verb *poiein*, to create – and if Tolkien does anything, he creates. The power of poetry perhaps lies in the way that it can linguistically and musically spark the imagination. If that is the case, then Tolkien's prose is at times as poetic as the most startling or breath-taking passages of the Romantic canon:

> And in that very moment, away behind in some courtyard of the City, a cock crowed. Shrill and clear he crowed, recking nothing of wizardry or war, welcoming only the morning that in the sky far above the shadows of death was coming with the dawn.
> And as if in answer there came from far away another note. Horns, horns, horns. In dark Mindolluin's sides they dimly echoed. Great horns of the North wildly blowing. Rohan had come at last. (*LotR,* 861)

Tolkien's choice and use of language here is every bit as deliberate as that of his Romantic forbears. He weaves together semantic patterns, chosen details and literary allusions to create a moment of eucatastrophe. Tolkien's choice of prose, we might argue, serves as a foil to such moments of lyrical or visionary clarity. In this, perhaps he goes a step further than the Romantics; while they focussed on keeping their sense of imagination in overdrive, Tolkien's prose more closely mimics the experience of reality: our lives are not overflowing with this kind of imaginative, eucatastrophic clarity – what Virginia Woolfe would call 'moments of being'. A prosaic exposition of an imaginary world therefore allows us to integrate more fully with its mundane experience and its moments of being – something that poetry does not always permit us.

Tolkien's prose is littered with such instances; almost invariably, he ties that sense of 'poetry' to the experience of eucatastrophe, as in this example from *The Two Towers*:

> 'Look, Sam!' [Frodo] cried, startled into speech. 'Look! The king has got a crown again!'
> The eyes were hollow and the carven beard was broken, but about the high stern forehead there was a coronal of silver and gold. A trailing plant with flowers like small white stars had bound itself across the brows as if in reverence for the fallen king, and in the crevices of his stony hair yellow stonecrop gleamed.
> 'They cannot conquer forever!' said Frodo. And then suddenly the *brief glimpse* was gone. The sun dipped and vanished, and as if at the shuttering of a lamp, black night fell. (*LotR* 727, emphasis mine)

This second passage is perhaps less spine-tingling than the first coming, as it does, not on a field of battle but really just in a field – but the power of imagination and its culmination in eucatastrophic glimpses of something beyond us is nevertheless outspoken. We are presented first with a microcosmic, personal experience of the power of imagination in Frodo's response to the natural world. In fact, his experience is so over-powering that it startles our troubled hobbit hero to speech, the verbs *cried* and *startled* strongly implying a moment of transcendence before we reach its verbal expression in 'The king has got a crown again!'. It is in the imagining of a crown – expressed delicately but evocatively in Tolkien's detailed attention to the natural world, where the flowers become 'small white stars' – that we are led to the moment of clarity: 'they cannot conquer forever'. Like a true

Romantic, Tolkien turns to the natural world and infuses it with a sense of the eternal so as to express the power of the imagination to lesson us in eternal things. But Tolkien is at pains to show the temporal nature of this experience: Frodo's 'brief glimpse' is gone as suddenly as it appeared, and a more prosaic diction (with the vanishing sun compared to a shuttered lamp) reinforces our sense that everyday experience always truncates the moments in which our imaginations are liberated to glimpse beyond it. The juxtaposition is heart-rending – but it is chiefly achieved through creative mastery of natural details.

As *The Lord of the Rings* nears its end, Tolkien's engagement with the natural world becomes a *tour de force* of pathetic fallacy. The road to Mordor becomes somewhat of a physical representation of Frodo and Sam's emotional and spiritual journey, heightening our sense of their exhaustion and nigh despair. Against this framework, Tolkien sets the scene for another moment of transcendent imagination:

> The land seemed full of creaking and cracking and sly noises, but there was no sound of voice or of foot. Far above Ephel Duath in the West the night-sky was still dim and pale. There, peeping among the cloud-wrack above a dark tor high up in the mountains, Sam saw a white star twinkle for a while. The beauty of it smote his heart, as he looked up out of the forsaken land, and hope returned to him. For like a shaft, clear and cold, the thought pierced him that in the end the Shadow was only a small and passing thing: there was light and high beauty for ever beyond its reach. (*LotR*, 957)

C. M. Bowra once wrote that: 'The Romantics... explore[d]... the world of the spirit... each of them believed in an order of things which is not that which we see and know... They wished to penetrate to an abiding reality... [and] were convinced that, though visible things are the instruments by which we view this reality, they are not everything and have indeed little significance unless they are related to some embracing and sustaining power'.[13] In this passage, Tolkien does just that.

The artistry and setting of the natural world have again become the vehicle for a powerful epiphany of imagination. Tolkien's language here oscillates, in a way that is delightfully appropriate to Samwise, between the touching tones of the everyday ('peeping', 'twinkle for a while') to the high and poetic modes of romance ('smote', 'forsaken'). Sam is aware both of the transience of the piercing star and the permanence of the idea it represents in his imagination. Tolkien perfectly captures the essence of a moment of divine vision as it occurs, not in the Romantic imagination, but in human experience – and, vitally, this linking of reality and the eternal leads to eucatastrophic renewal: hope returns to Sam so that 'his own fate, and even his master's, ceased to trouble him'.

The twinkling white star in every way indicates to us an embracing and sustaining power. This very Romantic capacity of using the natural world to capture the essence of spiritual moments is evident throughout Tolkien's work. The same imagination that conjures up wild worlds uses the very fabric of those worlds to transmit hope and imagination as best it can.

SHELOB'S LAIR: AN ASIDE ON TOLKIEN AND THE GOTHIC

Of course, the Romantic imagination did not simply conjure up instances of revelatory clarity. The movement was experiential and so also indulged in the sensuous and the nightmarish. The idealism

---

13. C. M. Bowra, *The Romantic Imagination*, Oxford Paperbacks, Oxford, 1976, p. 9.

of the Romantics gave rise to the thrills of the gothic – literature so radical that it was deemed unsuitable for women. While many of these works – such as *Frankenstein* or *Wuthering Heights* – are now considered among the classics of world literature, they were sensational and unpredictable.

The link between the monstrous and the world of Romance may well seem evident to us – knights were fighting dragons long before Spenser's Redcrosse knight encountered Errour in her den or Gawain ventured to the Green Chapel – but the radical nature of the Romantics produced an equally radical version of the monstrous. For some, the gothic quickly became viewed as a distasteful literary expression of excess, calculated to thrill and little else.

And here is another place where Tolkien differs from his Romantic and Gothic forbears: he wrote that 'every romance that takes things seriously must have a warp of fear and horror, if however remotely or representatively it is to resemble reality, and not the merest escapism.'[14] While acknowledging the integral link between romance and horror Tolkien's focus is still clearly that of resembling reality. In the same letter, he adds about the horror he has attempted in his own novel: 'But I have failed if it does not seem possible that mere mundane hobbits could cope with such things. I think that there is no horror conceivable that such creatures cannot surmount, by grace (here appearing in mythological forms) combined with a refusal of their nature and reason at the last pinch to compromise or submit.'[15]

For Tolkien, the purpose of fear and horror is to both render the world of the imagination more life-like, and to produce a platform

---

14. Humphrey Carpenter, ed., *The Letters of J. R. R. Tolkien*, with the assistance of Christopher Tolkien, HarperCollins, London, 1995, Letter 109, p. 120.

15. Op. cit., Letter 109, p. 120.

for the outworking of grace. This is perhaps seen nowhere as clearly as in Shelob's lair:

> In a few steps they were in utter and impenetrable dark... Here the air was still, stagnant, heavy, and sound fell dead [...] As they thrust forward they felt things brush against their heads, or against their hands, long tentacles or hanging growths perhaps... and still the stench grew.
> ... from behind them came a sound, startling and horrible in the heavy padded silence: a gurgling, bubbling noise, and a long venomous hiss. They wheeled round, but nothing could be seen. Still as stones they stood, staring, waiting for they did not know what.
> ... Then, as he stood, darkness about him and a blackness of despair and anger in his heart, it seemed to [Sam] that he saw a light: a light in his mind, almost unbearably bright at first, as a sun-ray to the eyes of one long hidden in a windowless pit...
> The bubbling hiss drew nearer, and there was a creaking as of some great jointed thing that moved with slow purpose on the dark. A reek came on before it. 'Master, master!' cried Sam, and the life and urgency came back into his voice. 'The Lady's gift! The star-glass!...'
> 'The star-glass?' muttered Frodo, as one answering out of sleep, hardly comprehending. 'Why, yes! Why had I forgotten it? A light when all other lights go out! And now indeed light alone can help us.' (*LotR*, 744 ff.)

Tolkien does not stint in building up the horror of Shelob's lair and is masterful in his execution of suspense. But where Peter Jackson unashamedly turns to the tropes of the horror-film (itself a genre drawing heavily on the gothic) Tolkien keeps the narrative details concrete and sense-focussed, drawing his readers into the lair itself. Like Frodo and Sam, we are left with only our senses of touch, sound and smell – literal and metaphorical sight only returns with the memory of Galadriel and the use of the star-glass. It is Galadriel's gift – that of light in the darkness – which acts as the grace that permits the hobbits to surmount the horror of Shelob's lair. Keeping his focus on overcoming horror rather than allowing it to overwhelm the narrative sets Tolkien apart from those who first followed in the steps of the Romantics.

The Great Instrument for the Moral Good

Shelley once wrote that the imagination was 'the great instrument for the moral good'. Although their interpretation of moral was not necessarily uniform the statement is summative of much that the Romantics strove to achieve. Imagination was a tool to enrich human experience.

Tolkien undeniably lived and wrote in the tail of the Romantics' visionary comet, and his work has traits in common. But in Tolkien's case, 'moral' good would perhaps be better read as spiritual good – for him, imagination is a pathway to the integration of the world around us with the world beyond us. It is when the two are imaginatively connected, allowing us through one to catch a glimpse of the other – when we are, as Tolkien puts it, escape and then return to the world able to see green as green again – that imagination has served its highest purpose. He strove to unify the realms of experience and 'being' in a way that encompassed the eternal but enriched, rather than cast aside, the temporal. Standing at the threshold between imagination and faith,

Tolkien's romanticism truly is a kind of divine vision.

A Star Above the Mast: Tolkien, Faërie and the Great Escape[1]

This paper purposes to examine the treatment of Faerie in a selection of Tolkien's minor works, with particular reference to Smith of Wootton Major, Leaf by Niggle, The Sea Bell and Bilbo's Last Song.

These works both explore and test facets of the relationship between man and faerie as exposited by Tolkien in 'On Fairy Stories', and, written under the shadow of the war or towards the end of his life, all share a tone of valediction or bereavement.

In addition to an initial examination of faerie, this paper's scope will be to study the ways in which faerie and farewells are interminably intertwined in Tolkien's works, both minor and as a whole, and how this, whilst playing a principal part in the formation of the minor works, also autobiographically reflects a sense that Tolkien had of his own time.

The glimpsing of other worlds is at the heart of faërie,[2] but at the heart of man is a deep-seated yearning for more than a glimpse; at the heart of man lies the desire for 'the Great Escape: the escape from Death'. (*OFS*, 68) This escape is figured in faërie by what Tolkien calls the sundered paths of the two kindred; to man is given the gift of death, and to the elves the gift of deathlessness. Tolkien posits that, just as our own storytelling traditions speak

---
1. First published in Margaret Hiley and Frank Weinreich, eds., *Tolkien's Shorter Works: Essays of the Jena Conference 2007*, Jena, 2008..

2. J.R.R. Tolkien, 'On Fairy Stories' in *Tree and Leaf*, HarperCollins, London, 2001, first published Allen and Unwin 1964, p. 41. All quotations from *OFS* are taken from this edition.

of the quest for eternal life and escape from death, the stories of the elves would be filled with escape from deathlessness. This notion was solidified in Tolkien's own mythology in the tale 'Of Beren and Lúthien', where the pivotal point of the myth is found in the escape from deathlessness chosen by Lúthien in the halls of Mandos.

That Lúthien's farewell to the world of faërie is at the beating heart of Middle-earth tells us something about how Tolkien viewed the great escape and the relationship between man and faërie.

Before we may venture to faërie, we must consider the assumption that man seeks a great escape even in our own time, and examine how faith and faërie may be linked.

Matters of faith have always dominated man's view of the world. If you look to the consolation provided by the great religions you will find the great escape presented as the afterlife; the place where, according to the Christian mythos, there will be 'no more mourning or crying.'[3] Seeking this escape ultimately entails leaving the world through death. But man has always sought other ways to reach the eternal world. In the Middle Ages many entered into the anchoritic life. These men and women felt that withdrawing from the world was a gesture of responsible fugitism which brought them closer to the great escape; seclusion from the world was best sought swiftly so as to come more quickly to the New Jerusalem. This style of life – rejecting the world by closeting oneself in a cell to contemplate the divine – could not be taken on lightly. Anchoritic 'guides' like the *Ancrene Wisse* figured the novice's withdrawal from our world as a battle against spiritual forces. In this, authors borrowed language from both the Bible and popular romances; the latter heavily influenced by the

---

3. *The Holy Bible New International Version*, Hodder & Stoughton, London, 2000, *Revelation* 21: 4.

traditions of faërie. Long before Tolkien wrote, faith and faërie were intertwined. Visions of the afterlife were touched by faërie, and vice versa.

So to faërie. You will find the great escape offered by faith foreshadowed in the perilous realm in the countless journeys of men who fall asleep upon a mound. Here, the fleeting (and at times joyous) escape is marred by farewells, both to the world on leaving it, and to faërie on returning. When travellers return, it is often to find that the long years of their lives have passed along with all whom they have known. The returned wanderer becomes doubly outcast; none can know him in his own world and he can never return to the realm of faërie where he once resided. Think for a moment of the fate of Keats' knight in *La Belle Dame sans Merci*, left 'alone and palely loitering'[4] by the withered sedge; his rest on a mound leaves him 'in thrall',[5] along with the dozens of kings, princes and warriors who have been beguiled before him. Having tasted the raptures of faërie he becomes a prisoner in the world, bereft of all his joy. The knight enters into a kind of involuntary anchorage, with his memories of the belle dame making his cell walls; rather than passing his time in prayer, he passes it pining for the eternal world that was shown to him in the guise of faërie.

We can compare this to the experience of the dreamer in the Gawain-poet's *Pearl*, a work later edited by Tolkien and E.V. Gordon.[6] In this poem, the boundaries of faith and faërie cross, co-existing in a way reminiscent of the mixed elements of paganism and Christianity in the epic poem *Beowulf*. The poem's dreamer, sleeping on a mound, does not encounter a belle dame nor even

---

4. John Barnard, ed., 'La Belle Dame sans Merci', *John Keats: The Complete Poems*, Penguin Books, Harmondsworth 1981, p.334.

5. Op. cit., p. 334.

6. E. V. Gordon, ed., *Pearl*, Clarendon Press, Oxford, 1980. All quotations from *Pearl* are taken from this edition.

descend to faërie, but rather ascends to a vision of the New Jerusalem where he meets again his 'pearl', posited to represent a daughter lost to him in death. The Pearl expounds the substance of this vision – a kind of catechism wherein the dreamer slowly grasps the promises of heaven - but the joy and consolation which he reaps are countered by his sudden reawakening into the primary or historical world where his grief returns to him in force. The dreamer can speak about what lies beyond the faërie-like 'crystal cliffs' (*Pearl*, 3.174) and river of his dream, but he must still live out his years on earth. Although he closes by enthusiastically expounding the theological essence of what he has learned, his farewell to his vision is a troubled one; his attempt at escape has been thwarted.

In *Pearl* we can see traces of Tolkien's theory of eucatastrophe; that faërie can be a means of highlighting faith, as the Pearl does when she speaks to the dreamer about the New Jerusalem. Though faërie cannot, as Tolkien observed, be 'the road to heaven' (*OFS*, 5), it possesses a haunting echo of that escape. So man, seeing in faërie aspects of the greater journey, ventures after it. Some are wounded in the search, others are enriched. What a man finds when he crosses the threshold is determined not so much by the realm where he travels, but what he takes with him.

It is this taut relationship between man and the perilous realm that Tolkien explores in so many of his minor works. In charting possible relationships between men and faërie, Tolkien tries to demonstrate the inherent value of faërie to men, and to reconcile it via eucatastrophe to the eternal world of the great escape.

So how does Tolkien illustrate these relationships? We may begin with a word of caution: 'while [a traveller] is [in faërie] it is dangerous for him to ask too many questions, lest the gates should be shut and the keys be lost' (*OFS*, 3). Tolkien knew, perhaps better than most, that the realm of faërie is called 'perilous' for good reason. Even (or especially) in childhood, we are well aware that faërie is high and deep, with creatures in its borders who purpose both good and evil. These stories teach us that those who travel into faërie with 'the heart of a little child' (*OFS*, 44), with humility and innocence, succeed in their trial, whatever its nature. But those who are arrogant – the hordes of elder princes and princesses whose youngest siblings outdo them – never come to a good end. For them, faërie is the idle realm of children.

In the minor works on which I have chosen to focus, Tolkien presents us with several types of people who approach faërie: first those who don't believe in faërie; second those that hold false beliefs about faërie and its nature; third people for whom faërie can be detrimental despite their knowledge of it; and fourth, figures who both believe in, and know, faërie. For this last group, knowledge of the perilous realm affects the kind of recovery, escape and consolation that Tolkien clarifies in 'On Fairy Stories'.

Characters with no belief in faërie hold that faërie is better spelt *ai* than *ae*, and that the stories are fit only for the entertainment of children. *Smith of Wootton Major*[7] presents us with just such a character: Nokes. He has been disabused of faërie, and actively seeks to diminish its influence on others. His notions of wands and pink icing, not to mention his sidelong snickers, clearly seek to relegate faërie to the nursery for 'it amuses the children' (*Smith*, 152). This is an activity that we know Tolkien found detestable, attributing it particularly to academics and critics, and comparing it to cutting off other adult arts by relegating them to the nursery (*OFS*, 35). In 'On Fairy Stories', Tolkien writes that 'the fear of the beautiful fay that ran through the elder ages almost eludes

---

7. J.R.R. Tolkien, 'Smith of Wootton Major' in *Tales from the Perilous Realm*, HarperCollins, London, 2002, pp. 147-178. All quotations from *Smith* are taken from this edition.

our grasp. Even more alarming: goodness is itself bereft of its proper beauty' (*OFS*, 65). This bereavement is a result of deeming faërie as childish, and results in losing any sense of awe. Nokes understands neither awe-full fear nor awe of goodness; for the characters in which we, as readers, see these attributes Nokes has only patronising words: Smith is a 'quiet, slow boy' (*Smith*, 173), Alf is 'nimble' and 'artful' (*Smith*, 178). Nokes deprecates faërie itself at every turn, as when he snidely asks Alf to tell him if, among the raisins for the cake, he notices any 'special, fairy ones' (*Smith*, 152). Nokes, unlike Smith, feels a pitiable, grovelling fear when confronted with the King of Faërie in his proper guise: he can only beg not to be harmed. His encounter with faërie does not clear Nokes' sight; he attributes his vision to bad food.

For Nokes, everything has been disenchanted. Yet whilst he pours scorn on faërie, he still reaches for its creative power although he does not apprehend its source: in the matter of the cake, he must rely on what he has garnered surreptitiously from Prentice to satisfy his 'severe critics' (*Smith*, 150). He claims a creative and inventive superiority to Prentice, saying that it is '[his] place to have ideas, and not [Prentice's]' (*Smith*, 153), but he can only palely copy Prentice's genius. Nokes has dethroned faërie, and seeks to be a 'master of arts' in its place.

We can easily apply to Nokes many of Tolkien's comments about those who advocated 'real life' over 'fantasy' (*OFS*, 63): factories and railways would be more real to Nokes than centaurs and dragons. In his subordination of faërie to the nursery and to 'real life', Nokes suffers a long-term bereavement which he cannot see himself, but which is represented in the pomposity of his character. His joy at the end of the tale that Prentice is 'gone at last' (*Smith*, 178) rings deadeningly in the reader's ears. For Nokes, there is no great escape; the greatest achievement in Wootton Major is the great riddance of Alf.

Smith of Wootton Major reveals Tolkien's anxiety at the critical treatment of faërie; Nokes' attitude expresses Tolkien's feeling that faërie was being reduced to nursery rhymes by critics who saw only escapism, not the great escape, in its borders. That Nokes' voice dominates the end of the text reflects this, and creates a feeling of bereavement. It is of note that this keen sense of loss appears in one of Tolkien's last works, at a time when his own thought was 'weighted with the presage of 'bereavement".[8] Tolkien's concern that the didactic qualities of faërie will be lost as the world fills with Nokeses is clear. It is just this bereavement that Nokes has suffered without knowing it.

Holding no belief in faërie is, as we have seen, bad enough. As a younger man, Tolkien had also studied what happened to men who held false beliefs about the perilous realm. His poem *The Looney* was first written in 1934, and later revised and republished in 1962 as *The Sea Bell*[9]. In both poems we can see Tolkien exploring another bereaving aspect of faerie, this time the result of seeking faërie and the great escape, but with that trademark of the great tragedies: hubris.

The most notable change between the two versions of Tolkien's poem is in terms of framing; originally, like Keats' *La Belle Dame*, the piece represented the speech of the titular Looney, who has returned from faërie and is recounting his misadventure to an interested party. But the later version has no comparable narrative frame. Instead, in the added introduction, it is noted that the poem (subtitled 'Frodo's Dreme'), is 'of hobbit origin' (Bombadil, 64). As Tom Shippey has noted in his book *Tolkien: Author of the*

---

8. Humphrey Carpenter, ed., *The Letters of J. R. R. Tolkien*, with the assistance of Christopher Tolkien, HarperCollins, London, 1995, Letter 389.

9. J.R.R. Tolkien, 'The Adventures of Tom Bombadil' in *Tales from the Perilous Realm*, HarperCollins, London, 2002, pp. 61-118. *The Sea Bell*: pp. 110-114. All quotations from *Bombadil* are taken from this edition.

Century, this notation calls our attention to an alternative ending[10] for Frodo where there is no great escape to Valinor.

Like Firiel in *The Last Ship*, *The Sea Bell*'s traveller encounters an empty ship. His call that 'it is later than late' (*Bombadil*, 110), brings to mind the great escape. The 'forgotten strand' (*Bombadil*, 110) where he disembarks, and to which we can compare later descriptions of the white shores of Valinor, is beautiful but deserted. To the traveller's horror, the landscape is not paradise regained but rather threatening; there are 'hidden teeth' (*Bombadil*, 110) in it, the willows weep, the flowers are like fallen stars, and the ford is guarded by 'gladdon swords' (*Bombadil*, 111). The traveller finds no one and wherever he goes, everything that he expects from faërie, figured in distant singing, flees from him. In response to this, the traveller makes himself a mantle and wand, claiming kingship for himself over the land. Having crowned himself with flowers he stands on a mound to make his proclamation of lordship, declaring himself master of the land and of its arts.

Though the traveller may have begun well by wishing to journey on the empty ship to seek the great escape, this gesture is obviously hubristic and misguided. Its arrogant nature is enhanced by the fact that in this deed the traveller effectively tries to force a second entry into faërie on his own terms; his mocking crown is an attempt to gain access to the hidden world which is frustratingly just beyond his reach. But when he tries to master faërie he becomes like a mole, bent to the ground. Rather than an escape his claim produces a shroud of night, and brings to him a kind of death that touches everything about him; Tolkien vividly describes the dead trees, filled with spiders and beetles. The traveller, unsurprisingly, wanders 'in wit' (*Bombadil*, 112) in this period where faërie lies dead all about him.

---

10. Tom Shippey, *J.R.R. Tolkien: Author of the Century*, HarperCollins, London, 2002, p. 282.

The traveller at last makes the long journey home. Returned from his escape, he casts away everything, including the sea bell which he will never more hear. The object has become a shell in more senses than one, and represents the hollowness of faërie for the traveller. His desperate experience in faërie was the result of forsaking the first image and true form of faërie (represented by the threatening sea and caves) for one of his own imagining (of hares and singing on the hill). These he never finds, even though faërie encompasses them. The traveller's hubristic experience outcasts him both from faërie and from his own world upon his return; the ships standing in the port are 'laden with light' (*Bombadil*, 113), at peace and fulfilled, while the returnee is 'dark as a raven' (*Bombadil*, 113), unfulfilled and bereft.

Tolkien's concern about having a correct attitude to faërie is clear; neither the realm nor tales of it may be trifled with, especially by means of adaptation or domination. The traveller seeks a very tame faërie and in his disappointment his farewell to it is bitter. He returns unable to speak of his journey to anyone, because, just as in faërie, none will speak to him. That Tolkien revised this poem later on in his life may illustrate some of Tolkien's own fears regarding his work; had he obscured the great escape in what he wrote? Had he trifled with faërie and rejected its true nature? *The Sea Bell* becomes an anti-faërie story. The arrogant rejection of the great escape and a true realm of faërie robs the traveller of the real world. The great escape has passed him by, the glimpse lost as the sea bell ceases to ring.

So trying to master faërie is a perilous business. How can we reconcile our visions of faërie to the real world, and all that the real world represents? Our world is full of business and toil and duty that cannot easily be set aside to search for faërie. For *The Sea Bell*'s traveller, that search entailed the loss of both faërie and of society in his own world. Is the risk one worth bearing, when we have so many duties and the price of adventure can be so great? Surely it is safer to be like Nokes, and allow faerie to pass.

Tolkien did not hold this view. In *On Fairy Stories* he expresses at length his notion that involvement with faërie was vital in facilitating and deepening ties to the real world rather than the opposite. We can compare this idea to that hinted at by C. S. Lewis in his Narnia stories, where the children gradually grow 'too old'[11] for the faërie realm of Narnia, but must take the lessons they have learned there back to their own world. So the experience of faërie, unlike that of *The Sea Bell*'s traveller, can be made a part of the real world. But the transition and reconciliation are not easy; for some, the perilous realm itself becomes dangerously greater than the escape that it mimics.

This concern is vividly expressed in *Leaf by Niggle*. In Niggle, Tolkien lays before us the unenviable position of a man unconvinced of his ability, and perhaps unable, to reconcile faërie and his duties in the primary world in his own lifetime. Faërie, and the great escape itself as figured in Niggle's journey, become distractions rather than a source of recovery or reflection of the eternal world.

Niggle is afraid of the great journey due to his fascination with faërie and knowledge that he often struggles to complete all the tasks allotted to him. Like the traveller in *The Sea Bell*, Niggle is possessive of his time in faërie; he spends a good deal of time painting, setting, for example, great importance on a single leaf at the expense of others. This obsession with faërie is never allowed to go so far that he does not participate in the real world, but he does so with the kind of heavy heart that: '[makes] him uncomfortable more often than it [makes] him do anything' (*LN*, 93). Niggle constantly feels pulled away from his love of faërie by the hindrances of the real world, whereas his love of faërie should

---

11. C.S. Lewis, *Prince Caspian*, Penguin, Harmondsworth, 1962, p. 188.

actually fuel his involvement in it (just as, we might add, a looking forward to the 'great escape' should sharpen our taste for our own world).

Unlike *The Sea Bell*'s traveller or Smith, Niggle is not offered a journey to faërie: the journey offered to him is death itself. It is little wonder, then, that he is trying to put it off as best as he can reasoning that once dead, his own voyage to faërie, figured in his painting, will be concluded. He sees no link between faerie, his world, and the great escape. For Niggle, faërie is both a distraction and a frustration. It is not until he learns to place the beauty of faërie and the real world together during his purgatorial sojourn with the mysterious voices and subsequent work with Parish that his connection to faërie bears real fruit. It is then that his painting reflects part of the great journey, becoming the very landscape in which he travels: *Niggle's Parish*.

Here, Tolkien very clearly states that the subcreation of those who can describe faërie can also reflect the great journey. The conclusion to Niggle's story is an antidote to the despair at the end of The Sea Bell. Tolkien also suggests that those who long for faërie, like Niggle, look for the great escape in another guise. For many, we are told, Niggle's painting 'makes the best introduction to the mountains' (*LN*, 118); that is to say, the crystal cliffs of the eternal world.

In Niggle's story we can see that it is possible to come to some kind of understanding with faërie, and that faërie itself can be the connection between the historical and eternal worlds. This connection is also at the heart of Tolkien's eucatastrophe, the moment when the eternal world strikes through into the historical one. According to Tolkien, faërie was the best kind of setting for this occurrence, and it goes without saying that Tolkien hoped that his own work could have a similar affect. Niggle only comprehends this aspect of his painting after his journey has begun; his relationship with faërie is retrospective. We can posit that the ideal would be to be reconciled to faërie whilst in the historical world, allowing it to enrich and prepare us for the greater journey. Interestingly, the minor work that best demonstrates this positive relationship with faërie is also the one that speaks most clearly about the loss that accompanies faerie: *Smith of Wootton Major*.

Smith is able to pass freely between the real world and faërie (a feat making him nigh on unique in literature) thanks to the fay star. This star enriches Smith deeply; compare, for example, Smith's ability in song, and the beauty of the practical things that he makes, to Niggle's frustrated efforts at a double life. Smith travels in faërie and sees things both terrible and lovely, but, unlike Nokes or *The Sea Bell*'s traveller, he remains in awe of them, does not flee from them, and does not attempt to claim lordship over them. He seeks the King of faërie, rather than seeking to become the king, and in return is guarded from the 'greater evils' (*Smith*, 157). He remains a learner and explorer, and his encounters with faërie give him a great shadow, noted by his son as the true measure of his character. He grows beyond his stature in Wootton Major, but does not outgrow the village. He is at peace both in faërie and at home, respected in both places.

The greatest moment of Smith's journey is when he is greeted by and recognises the Queen of faërie. But this moment, which shows the depth of Smith's connection to faërie, also highlights his bereavement from it:

> So he seemed to be both in the World and in Faery, and also outside them, and surveying them, so that he was at once in bereavement, and ownership, and in peace. When after a while the stillness passed he raised his head and stood up. The dawn was in the sky and the stars were pale, and the Queen was gone [...] and he knew that his way now led back to bereavement. (*Smith*, 164)

Here Tolkien summarises the double-nature of knowing faërie, highlighting at once the way that faërie figures the great escape, but also how it is not, and cannot be, that escape. The paradox of being both in bereavement and ownership is something that reaches beyond the scope of experience in the primary world, and is heightened by faërie. Smith's true bereavement is in attaining for a moment the clarity loaned to faërie by its echo of the great escape, and knowing that he cannot keep it, just as he cannot keep the star. He must bid it farewell.

Like Bilbo giving up the Ring, Smith gives up the star of his own volition, knowing that some things are not given as heirlooms. Thus, he renounces the possession of *The Sea Bell*'s traveller, and in so doing he demonstrates a nobility which is akin to faërie. His return to Wootton Major is similar to that of Sam in *The Lord of the Rings*; Smith will do much good to the world by being back in it. Smith's son notes that Smith has much to teach besides the working of iron, but a shadow of the journeys that he made will always lie over him, making him more than what he would otherwise have been. Smith keeps the hall gilded in memory of Alf, just as Sam keeps the Red Book.

In Smith we see the epitome of a man touched by faërie, but we see also that faërie must always be left. For Smith, unlike Frodo and even Sam, there is no last crossing to Elvenhome, though he likely longs for it. Like the dreamer in *Pearl*, Smith must content himself with the memory of his journey while awaiting the greater one. Smith in many ways represents an ideal link to faërie, but his farewell to it does not yet entail the complete reconciliation between faërie and the historical world that Tolkien longed for. It is the sorrow in parting from faërie having glimpsed, but not attained, the great escape that creates the sense of 'an old man's book'[12] in many of Tolkien's minor works.

---

12. Op. cit. [8], Letter 389.

We have seen how possible relationships with faërie can vary from arrogance and blatant disbelief, to eventual understanding of and acquiescence to bereavement and farewell. It is at the point of farewell that the true nature of the relationship is put to the test; for some, the mimetic nature of faërie offers escape, recovery and consolation so as to effect a fruitful return to our own world. Tolkien's theory of eucatastrophe puts both reader and author in the place of the king who, after long and wild adventures in faërie, returns to his kingdom with clear and deepened sight because he has glimpsed the eternal in his journey. The manner of our return reflects the nature of our journey, and our deepened sight should give us the vision to look forward to the journey for which faërie has been a kind of testing ground. Like Smith, we should have the courage to keep the hall gilded in a world beset with Nokeses.

Tom Shippey views Smith as a 'valedictory address',[13] and certainly there is in Smith much that bears comparison to Tolkien himself. There is the long history of travel in faërie, the illustration of its scope in the dark elves, the dancing queen, and the weeping birch. In Smith himself many of Niggle's worrying faults have been remedied; his participation in the life of Wootton Major is enhanced by his sojourns in faërie, and perhaps Tolkien felt able to say the same of his own work. After Smith's return to Wootton Major it is difficult to know what the village's future will be, but it is at least encouraging that any of the children seem 'fit to find the star' (*Smith*, 176). Perhaps one of the consolations of Tolkien's own farewell lay in the notion that his journeys would help to encourage a correct attitude towards faërie, and through that towards the great escape.

For Tolkien, faërie was a place where the great escape to the eternal world was foreshadowed. But in many of Tolkien's works,

---

13. Op. cit. [10], Tolkien, p. 303.

both major and minor, there is a tone of despair, as travellers are forced to return to the historical world, some without learning the lessons that faërie had to teach them. There is, however, one of Tolkien's minor works where faith and faërie collide at the very departure point of the great escape: *Bilbo's Last Song*.[14]

The poem has at its beginning the weight of impending bereavement figured in the familiar motif of the ending day, except in Bilbo's case it has already ended, and his eyes are 'dim' (*BLS*, 1). The singer bids farewell to his friends; like many before him, he can hear the call of a world beyond his own, and the stanza moves between literal descriptions of the harbour (the stony wall and the salt-sea) to visionary statements of going 'beyond the sunset' (*BLS*, 6). The stanza's focus on what the singer can hear, compounded by the emphasis on dimness of sight, enhances the capacity for vision that reaches beyond the world, just as those who go to faërie see beyond it. But, on the cusp of the great journey, this vision can no longer be sneered at.

The second stanza returns to literal descriptions of the moorings fretting (perhaps with a desire to begin the journey). Yet as the stanza moves on, the searing vision of the first stanza settles into a kind of travelogue, charting the road that must be taken through shadows to 'west of West' (*BLS*, 15). In the final line we are told that in these lands night 'is quiet and sleep is rest' (*BLS*, 16). This draws on the biblical assurance of a future where there will be no more weeping; the visionary world, enhanced by faërie, is beginning to echo the eternal one.

In the third stanza the poem mentions the Lonely Star, in which we can see the crossroads both of faërie and eternity. This star is now no longer a passport as it was for Smith; it is the guide, and the true measure of the journey is where the singer, whose

---

14. J.R.R. Tolkien, Bilbo's Last Song, Hutchison, London, 2002. All quotations from *BLS* are taken from this edition.

eyes had previously been dim, cries to the ship 'I see the Star above your mast!' (*BLS*, 24). To this point, the poem has been a vision of the great escape and the way to the West, but now, in this eucatastrophic moment, the Star itself is seen. Faërie and the great escape are unified as the star, laid down in old age, returns as a guide to lead the singer home.

That the star at this point of farewell stands for both faith and faërie is a fitting conclusion to Tolkien's long life. This double-facet of the star also ties *Bilbo's Last Song* to Tolkien's essay 'On Fairy Stories', where he states that faërie stories moved closest to the eternal world in their capacity for eucatastrophe. For Tolkien, who struggled in many of his works to reconcile faërie to the real world, the long-sought great escape shows that both faërie and faith unite at last west of West, in the star above the mast. He finds himself gazing at the very core of eucatastrophe: an 'especially beautiful fairy-story' that is 'primarily true' (*OFS*, 72). What greater escape could there be?

'An Old Light Rekindled: Tolkien's Influence on Fantasy'[1]

The fantasy genre has long been the subject of awe, adoration, revulsion and repulsion in equal and discriminatory measures. The genre has been present as long as mankind has told tales, and brings with it a collection of expected tropes, topoi, stereotypes and themes. Considering the nature and roots of the genre, the literary climate in which Tolkien was received and the 'master of fantasy's' own aims from the perspective of a critic and writer, this paper asks what expectations Tolkien has bound upon the genre and how far it is possible for his literary descendents to write in (or away from) his shadow. It traces the links between influence and originality, examining Tolkien's goals of sub- creation and eucatastrophe, asking whether these are the lynch-pins of fantasy and what, ultimately, constitutes Tolkien's legacy to the genre that he re-ignited.

> The first qualification for judging any piece of workmanship from a corkscrew to a cathedral is to know what it is – what it was intended to do and how it was meant to be used.[2]

The term 'fantasy' has a disconcerting plurality of meaning with, it seems, as many semantic facets as the worlds and subgenres it has

---

1. First published 'Tolkien's Influence on Fantasy', in *Hither Shore Band 9 2012*, DTG, 2012.
2. C.S. Lewis, *A Preface to Paradise Lost*, Atlantic Publishers and Distributors, Dehli, 2005, p. 1.

spawned. Certainly, the term is contemporarily associated with the 'faculty or activity of imagining improbable things' (OED) and is as much suggestive of 'an idea with no basis in reality' (OED) as it is a genre of fiction.

To address the question of Tolkien's influence on the genre we must first find our way through the ghost lights of awe, adoration, revulsion and repulsion that surround it – a quest well suited to the genre's scope – to ascertain something of what it is.

Fantasy: Penning The Black Sheep

The Oxford Dictionary of Literary Terms is intriguingly brief on the matter of fantasy, advising the reader to seek a more detailed exploration of the term in other sources. Indeed, it is almost as eloquent on the subject of 'ficelle'[3] as it is this troublesome genre. Critically speaking, fantasy is the black sheep of literature, sharing the fate that has befallen fairy tale's countless dispossessed princes and youngest daughters - it has often been overlooked and disinherited from the literary canon, deemed as of no more worth than 'juvenile trash'.[4] We might say that it is difficult to pen, both in terms of writing and containment.

So, what is fantasy? In his work *Other Worlds: The Fantasy Genre*, John H. Timmerman gives a handy list of six attributes that can be said to characterise a work of fantasy: 'the use of traditional *Story*, the depiction of *Common Characters and Heroism*, the evocation of another *World*, the employment of *Magic and the Supernatural*, the revelation of a *Struggle between Good and Evil*,

---

3. A term used by Henry James to describe a fictional character whose role as a confidante is exploited as a means of providing the reader with information while avoiding direct address from the narrator.
4. Edmund Wilson, 'Oo, Those Awful Orcs!', The Nation 182 (1956), 312–14.

and the tracing of a *Quest*.[5]

For Timmerman, these elements and motifs grant the genre a position at centre- stage of the literary tradition. They are certainly the elements which we would associate with Tolkien, Lewis, Williams, LeGuin, and other fantasists. Mark any work of 'fantasy' against these posts - from Sedgewick's *My Swordhand is Singing* to Hearn's *Tales of the Otori*, from George R.R. Martin's *A Game of Thrones* series to my own recently published novel, then the reader will find that these six attributes are generally unfailingly addressed.

We discern these elements, and their consequent concerns with morality, reality and truth, at the heart of the genre. W.H. Auden was in agreement that the quest played a central role in Tolkien's work, using it as a link between *The Lord of the Rings* and forbear texts such as Malory's *Morte D'Arthur*; C.S. Lewis weighed Tolkien against the imaginative scope of Ariosto. The link to writers like Ariosto and Spenser leads us suggestively to the moral complex of allegory and parable, but Tolkien argued that the genre's value here was not in its allegory but its 'applicability'.

Most readers would be hard pressed to deny the weight of this argument. Though, when taken to excess, applicability may lead to obsession (a fanaticism which the fantasy genre overtly attracts) through the temptation to completely absorb oneself in a fictional reality, the inherent applicability of fantasy to our own lives seems to be a crucial element of the genre's success – we might add it as a seventh element to Timmerman's six.

The question of applicability is relevant not only to Tolkien but to more modern works. Weighing boy wizard against high school teen, Robin Brown observes that: '*Harry Potter* is about confronting fears, finding inner strength and doing what is right

---

5. John H. Timmerman, *Other Worlds: The Fantasy Genre*, Bowling Green University Press, Bowling Green OH, 1983, p. 3.

in the face of adversity. *Twilight* is about how important it is to have a boyfriend'.[6] The concerns of one text pale in applicability compared with the other. Perhaps this is why Rowling's fantasy abides whilst Meyer's popularity only really soars with a limited and specific audience – the fantastic world of Harry Potter is imminently more applicable to the lives of its readers, whatever their age.

Putting aside all the subgenres of fantasy – high fantasy, sword and sorcery, urban fantasy, the marvellous, the uncanny, the fantastic – it seems that the universally recognisable structure of fantasy makes it a genre onto which we can – and desire to – project ourselves and our lives, applying our experience to the imaginary and the experience of fantasy's heroes to our own reality in a kind of didactic exchange. It is a liminal genre with immense power, opening the doors between faerie and reality.

Of course, these have been the attributes of the genre as long as we have told tales: as Tolkien would write in a letter to *The Observer* in 1938, fantasy in general (and his own writing in particular), is 'derived from (previously digested) epic, mythology and fairy-story'.[7] The key elements of fantasy can be traced back through the same illustrious literary heritage that produced the visionary scope of *Paradise Lost*, the fairy-tale redemption of Leontes in *The Winter's Tale* and the questioning of Chanticleer's digestive tract; we see them in the adventures of Odysseus, the founding of Rome, the battles of Beowulf, the journey of Gawain, the splintering of Camelot, the solitary way from Eden. Elements of fantasy are embedded in the foundations not only of the western narrative tradition but, as Joseph Campbell has identified,

---

6. R.B. Durham, *Twilight: An Unofficial Companion*, Lulu.com, Online, 2015, p. 6.

7. Humphrey Carpenter, ed., *The Letters of J. R. R. Tolkien*, with the assistance of Christopher Tolkien, HarperCollins, 1995, London, 1995, Letter 25, p. 31.

mythologies from across the world.[8]

It seems that we are hard-wired for this kind of storytelling – and it could be argued that no writer, not even the most postmodern or counter-cultural, can escape the themes and influence of fantasy: work from the trenches echoes the titanic clash of classical titans and struggle of man with destiny; Angela Carter's The Bloody Chamber and The Magic Toyshop operate on common cultural memory and expectations – crossing, like many fairy-tales and darker or gothic works of fantasy, into the macabre – and still Bettelheim's theory holds.[9] We read these stories to learn about ourselves and the world we live in.

ON THE BRINK: TOLKIEN'S PLACE

We have grappled for an understanding of the weave of this genre. Let us shift the shuttle towards Tolkien, and his particular place in it. Tolkien's passion, as a reader and storyteller, was 'ab initio for myth... and for fairy-story, and above all for heroic legend on the brink of fairy-tale and history' of which he perceived there is 'far too little in the world'.[10] He was the ideal audience for fantasy, recognising in his statement the composite elements of the genre. He believed throughout his life that fairy story 'is really an adult genre, and one for which a starving audience exists',[11] lamenting the 'false and accidental... connexion in the modern mind between children and 'fairy stories' '.[12] It might indeed be true to say that much of the antagonism towards Tolkien's work, and the fantasy genre in general, is the belief that it is 'inferior' and only suitable for children. Hand in hand with this goes the belief that fantasy

---

8. Joseph Campbell, *The Hero with A Thousand Faces*, New York, 1949.
9. Bruno Bettelheim, *The Uses of Enchantment*, London, 1976.
10. Op. cit. [7], Letter 131, p. 144.
11. Op. cit. [7], Letter 159, p. 209.
12. Op. cit. [7], Letter 163, p. 216.

is somehow a genre in which an author 'indulge[s] himself in developing the fantasy for his own sake'.[13]

Like many works of fantasy to follow it, Tolkien's work has polarised readers; many take a judgement on the genre based on one novel. When 'types' of readers and fantasy literature are so divergent, it is little wonder that the genre can come into ill-repute; a reader hungering after the masculine world of *Conan the Barbarian* may find little to attract them in *LotR*; the reader that adored the religious and moral themes woven into the Narnia stories may find the much more pagan archipelago of Earthsea difficult to swallow. As Tolkien observed, 'something of the teller's own reflections and 'values' will inevitably get worked in[to their tale]',[14] and, perhaps more than any other genre, the bounds of fantasy are so broad that there is as much to repel as enthral its readers.

GENRE-MAKER: TOLKIEN'S INFLUENCES

It should be noted, at this juncture, that Tolkien himself never called his work a work of fantasy – always (in a reflection of his own 'values') of fairy-story. He had felt called, from his earliest youth, to 'kindle a new light, or, what is the same thing, rekindle an old light in the world ... to testify for God and Truth'.[15] As his work On Fairy-Stories was to explore at length, for him 'fairy story' – what we might now call high fantasy – was the most exquisite vehicle of expression available to him for this purpose: it has 'its own mode of reflecting 'truth', different from allegory or sustained satire, or 'realism', and in some ways more powerful'.[16]

---

13. Op. cit [4].
14. Op. cit. [7], Letter 181, p. 233.
15. Op. cit. [7], Letter 5, p. 10.
16. Op. cit. [14].

Tolkien saw his own work as a continuation of a literary tradition that had been growing for hundreds of years.

And his influence? Influence, a word deriving from a Latin root meaning 'flowing into something', intends ways in which a writer has wrested an idea or genre in a particular direction. Some elements of Tolkien's influence on fantasy are clear and obvious not just in literature but also in media as diverse as art, film-making, role-playing games and MMO RPGs like *World of Warcraft* – where you can meet dwarves, elves and tree-people.

It doesn't just stop with the stock characters – Tolkien's influence is so pervasive that he has even altered our perception of the correct plural of 'dwarf'; a glance at dictionaries in circulation before *LotR* gained popularity (in my case, a dictionary from 1816) shows that the canonical plural was 'dwar*fs*'; now, the OED lists 'dwar*ves*' as an acceptable alternative and this is due to Tolkien's own 'private piece of bad grammar'.[17] Just imagine if he had had his wish, and gone with the delightful word 'dwarrows'.

Bringing dwarves and Elves – not as dainty, sylvan creatures but as formidable and powerful beings – to the fore of the genre, Tolkien directly challenged the prevailing Victorian views of fairies, and the overtly 'lavish ... fantastical, incoherent and repetitive' faerie he felt was portrayed in Arthurian romances.[18] He took these creatures straight back to their mythical northern roots, returning to them something perilous about their stature, something threatening to mankind. A reflection of this can be seen in Smith's encounter with the terrifying dark Elves in *Smith of Wootton Major*.

Perhaps modern fantasy writers have not always preserved the grandeur and terrifying enchantment of characters like Galadriel, but elements of the power and mystique that Tolkien gave them

---

17. Op. cit. [7], Letter 17, pp. 23–24.
18. Op. cit. [7], Letter 131, p. 144.

have trickled into later fantasy in the common portrayal of Elves as aloof and alluring. And, certainly, we expect to meet elves and dwarves in works of fantasy. Another stock character introduced by Tolkien is the orc – prior to his work, goblins and gnomes were about as close as you could get (and gnomes now seem to be merging into the trope of 'hobbit' that Tolkien introduced, as a race of generally innocent creatures attuned to nature and more concerned with the mundane than the concerns of the 'higher' fantasy races). The orc has been stewed in the public consciousness long enough that it is moving beyond its Tolkienian type, and beginning to make outings as a protagonist in its own right – as, for example, in the novel *Orcs*, or as a character class in the game 'Munchkin'.

Go into any bookshop to the fantasy section, and you will see another area of influence: maps. While Robert E. Howard had a rudimentary map at the beginning of his *Conan* novels, after Tolkien a map at the beginning of your work of fantasy is almost a prerequisite of the genre - and many examples of this *sine qua non* have the good guys in the western part of the landmass. Closely linked to this as a way of building a believable secondary world is the concept of sub-created languages – after Tolkien, any self-respecting fantasy author cannot simply talk about over-hearing a 'barbarian tongue', or scribble down some gibberish words and hope that the reader will suspend their disbelief. There is an expectation of (and perhaps a tolerance for) invented languages that was not present before Tolkien brought his work to the genre.[19]

---

19. For example, in the Conan Chronicles, speakers of other languages speak in 'a barbarian tongue'; it is also the stock of fairy tale and myth that when the protagonists meet a foreigner it may be mentioned that another tongue is spoken, but they do not use it. Perhaps we might look to the *Star Trek* franchise as an interesting modern comparison – Klingon was not developed as a full language until the late 70s, a number of years after Tolkien's work had gained popularity. Prior to this, Klingons always

An area of key concern in the fantasy genre is the role of women and female characters; Tolkien was annoyed by the criticism that *LotR* had 'no Women'[20] – Peter Jackson's adaptation was similarly raked. Let us not forget who defeated the Witch King at the battle of the Pelennor fields, and who tore down Sauron's stronghold with song where an Elven king had failed. Rather than saying that there are no women in Tolkien's work it would perhaps be fairer to say that there are no women who have been brushed with the values of feminism. In this, Tolkien could be said to differ substantially to those who have followed him in the genre. Tolkien's women are fewer far than men, but this is internally consistent to the pseudo-mediaeval reality he creates. Writers who choose to depict sexually liberated, sword-wielding warrior princesses are dealing with a different kind of sub-creation to Middle Earth; we might wonder whether even this is partly due to Tolkien's influence in the sense that it is a backlash against the more traditional, 'fairy-tale'-like conception of a woman's role.

Another element of Tolkien's influence is the attribution to him of the 'father of fantasy' title – which seems to be another way of saying that his works may be mercilessly pulped and regurgitated. *The Forgotten Realms* and *Shannara* series novels seem to be little more than a shameless ripping-off of their source material: my husband observes that 'they are to *LotR* what MacDonalds is to a restaurant'. Harsh, perhaps, but many Tolkien purists would agree with him. There is a fine line to be trodden here between the pulp-mill fiction that churns out poorly written novels simply because they will sell, and works that genuinely are 'the next J.R.R. Tolkien'. The trouble with these novels, all undoubtedly influenced by Tolkien, is that the question of their quality is down

---

spoke English. In contrast, *Babylon 5*, a science fiction series of the 90s, has alien languages built into its fabric from the outset.

20. Op. cit. [7], Letter 165, p. 220.

to the taste of the individual reader – returning us neatly to the problem of the audience of fantasy and the impact of that variable on the genre.

Tolkien's influence is also discernable in the way that he, and elements of his work, have been parodied – Terry Pratchett satirises and parodies the tropes of the fantasy genre and the writers who would model themselves too closely on the grand master. Others have not been so subtle – see, for example, the infamous *Bored of the Rings*. Others do away with Tolkien's tropes almost entirely – but even *The Princess Bride* does not move away from its 'fantastic' fairy tale origins.[21]

Perhaps the element of influence that most clearly unifies high fantasy or Tolkien's faerie is the pre-modern concept of the struggle of good versus evil. After the watershed of modernism and post-modernism, notions of a moral struggle founded in a sense of absolute right or wrong were considered unrealistic, disproven by the gritty reality of human experience. Black and white is too simplistic for modernism; fractured narrative and mores become the lynchpin of literature. Consequentially, moral 'greyness' is the shade very much in vogue even in fantasy. Modern works like *A Game of Thrones* seem to be more epic modernist fantasy than fantasy in Tolkien's much older sense. Tolkien's fantasy is high fantasy, a fantasy whose defining feature is an underlying moral matrix played out both macro and microcosmically, personally and universally. Tolkien knew he was the old light, knew that fantasy was shading away from black and white to grey. His work boldly rekindled a fading fascination with war in the heavenlies and the concept of an absolute moral compass. Perhaps contemporary fantasists, whether they echo this system of high fantasy or not, are

---

21. Excellent and entertaining material on the tropes of fantasy is available at <http://tvtropes. org/ pmwiki/pmwiki.php/Main/Fantasy> [accessed 12 November 2015].

equally indebted to Tolkien; where one mirrors, the other repulses. The influence remains – and so does the struggle to be noticed in the company of the master.

Combing through the 'good' and 'bad' examples of the fantasy genre – by necessity a subjective activity – it seems that, whether or not the individual work owes a great deal to Tolkien, a distinction emerges whereby influence and originality are balanced. A good piece of literature in any genre will doubtless be influenced by its forbears – such is the nature of human experience – but it will also offer newly-framed insights from a sub-created world. The form may well, like Tolkien's, be in fairy story or high fantasy – but if this is the origin rather than the goal, then the genre is taking steps in the right direction – steps on the same path as Tolkien himself.

THE TROPE CODIFIER

Tolkien has certainly become what the TV Tropes website calls the 'Trope Codifier' for high fantasy, 'the template that all later uses of the trope follow'. Did he ever intend this outcome? By desiring to 'rekindle an old light in the world', we could argue that Tolkien's purpose was very much to influence the direction and ideals of a genre. For him, though, this rekindling was not in characters or plot or the supernatural – or in any of the mechanics of fantasy. It was in the intention of it. To rekindle the old light, he brought his concept of eucatastrophe to the fore of his critical theory and his own writing. Fairy story was a way of bringing comfort and renewed vision to its readers, a way of bringing a suggestion of the transcendence and immanence of God back into the primary, historical world. To do this, Tolkien relied on sub-creation – the inner consistency of reality, and the unique conveyance afforded to him by another world. He recognised, however, the perils of this calling. *Leaf by Niggle* and *Smith of Wootton Major* clearly show Tolkien's concerns about being a writer of fantasy: Niggle struggles to balance his sub-creation with his duties to the primary world; Smith must ultimately relinquish the pleasures and perils of faerie to another. The sub-created world must be handled with care, as either a writer or a reader, or it becomes the flight of the deserter and abode of the fanatic.

It is in the element of sub-creation – creating another fantastical world – that many writers are ultimately paralleled to Tolkien. This capacity of envisioning another world is crucial to the concept of fantasy, lying in its Greek roots *phantatastikos*, meaning 'to have visions' or 'make visible'. But perhaps, unless a work of fantasy strives, as Tolkien did, to testify to truth by means of that sub-creation, the work falls vacuous and dead in the reader's hands. The true measure of high fantasy may be in its eucatastrophic quality – and this is in the area in which Tolkien is unparalleled.

THE SAME STORY STILL: WRITING IN TOLKIEN'S SHADOW

At this point, I proceed in my reflections not as a critic, but as a writer. In *LotR*, Samwise comes to the startling realisation that he and Frodo are still in the same, grand story of Middle Earth as Beren and Lúthien and dozens of heroic forbears. When you are a writer of fantasy, being in 'the same story' as Tolkien is something it is desperately hard to avoid.

I was introduced to Tolkien as a child of about seven, when my father read *The Hobbit* to my sister and me. I was enthralled – some of my most vivid memories are of my father's delight as he read to us 'Out of the frying pan, and into the fire'. The appeal of Middle-Earth was that it was another world – a world where I experienced joy and fear, grief and renewal. It formed my vision and understanding of the fantastic. My reading diet, from then on, constituted fairy stories, *The Arabian Nights*, *The Chronicles of Prydain*, *The Belgariad*, *The Derynii Chronicles*, *The Chronicles of Narnia*, the *Earthsea* quintet ...

When I first took up the pen at the tender age of eleven, I was reading *LotR*. I was stuck in the middle of Lothlórien (having been traumatised by the death of Gandalf and so terrified of Galadriel and her purposes for Frodo that I could read no further). Despite all my other reading, before and since, it was Tolkien's work that showed the strongest influence on my own, and was certainly foremost in my mind when I began writing. As all children do, I modelled myself on my 'master'. I left no trope un-copied; I had fearsome black riders pursuing a girl and her companions who were on a quest to preserve a magical medallion from the hands of an evil overlord who lived in a grand, black tower. Sound familiar? But you have to learn the craft from somewhere.

Over a number of years, an invented kingdom grew up as a background for these stories. The painfully patent similarities continued: I had elves and dwarves (who hated each other), and my group of heroes travelled the kingdom before being separated and having to continue their quest without the knowledge that their companions were alive. Evil defeated, they would be reunited. There was now, as my reading grew broader, some variation from my master's themes – I experimented with killing off principal characters and *not* bringing them back, and the avenues opened by a powerful and seductive villainess. Even so, these tales of Azzanor never truly removed themselves from Tolkien's shadow – and I was not yet aware that they should do so.

The next incarnation of my writing took me a step further away, and these tales – *The Chronicles of the Demonbane* – while still pitting heroes in a quest of light against dark, took on a more complex hue. Even so, they were the work of a youth still much too much influenced by Tolkien. I wanted to achieve what he had achieved – an internally consistent secondary reality – where I could tell a story about things that really mattered to me.

It was this series of stories that I first tried to publish. When rejected, I did not at first understand why. I ceased writing while I went to university and became a critic – of literature and of Tolkien's work. Through my studies I came to understand the terrible power of his influence – especially over me. He was the tree of fantasy, and I but a stunted leaf. To become truly like my hero of fantasy writing, I perceived that I had to become original – but there was nothing original that I could do. I continued to believe this until, walking to lectures one crisp spring morning, I came across a tree not far from the English department. From the wrung and settled branches, a spry, fresh, green leaf was budding. And I realised then that originality inherently springs from influence.

My ideas and values were turned with the sharpened perspective of adulthood back to the fantasy genre. I made my peace with Tolkien. Through my critical work, for my undergraduate degree and principally for these conferences, I came to understand more and more about the role of fantasy. Like Tolkien, I believe in its inherently eucatastrophic nature – that this genre is a platform where we can explore the issues and events that ultimately matter in the primary world. This was the kind of story I wanted to tell – and there were still stories to be told. I had to understand Tolkien, and acknowledge his influence, before I could focus on taking a step in the genre. My sub-creation has, in its own way, been a way of testifying to the same truth: fantasy is for the adult-minded and sharpens our taste for our own world – lessons that I only really learnt by interacting with 'the master of fantasy', both his imaginative and critical work.

Did I find originality? That is a question best left to my readers. But I believe that I have held true to the principle of fantasy that Tolkien held the dearest – telling a story with applicability. In my sub-created world,[22] the River Realm, a traditional story – the return of a dispossessed king – takes place against the backdrop

---

22. Anna Thayer, *The Traitor's Heir: Volume One of The Knight of Eldaran*, Austin and MacAuley, London, 2011.

of a battle of light and dark that is at times supernatural. So far, so fantasy. But there are no elves and dwarves, dragons, orcs, or devilish phantasmagorias. Only humans. The narrative is focalised through an everyman character whose personal journey is not always tied to the fate of the realm – in fact, critics may argue (and some readers have) that he is no hero at all. But who of us are? The fantasy genre is not just the preserve of peasants being unveiled as kings – it is a place where the choices ordinary people face every day can be questioned and explored.

INFLUENCE, OR INFLUENZA?

Whichever way we look at it, Tolkien's works, both academic and imaginative, have had an enormous influence over the unfolding of the genre that has followed him. I attest to that personally, and know many fantasy writers would say the same.

Tolkien was entirely cogent of the possibility of his work influencing others, feeling that: 'the cycles [of his tales] should be linked to the majestic whole, and yet leave scope for other minds and hands, wielding paint and music and drama'.[23] Those who consider him to have cast an unalterable shadow over the fantasy genre may feel that his influence is more of an influenza – that there is no place left for the genre to go, that we are destined to endless tales of hobbits and Elves that will never equal the work of the man whose imagination gobbled up every avenue of fantasy left.

But the truth is that Tolkien's overarching influence actually brought key aspects of this genre to the very forefront of study, and in his appeal to so many of us he has forced the academic world to look again at fantasy. His masterful re- weaving of crucial elements of story, and deeply considered theory of the vitality of

---

23. Op. cit. [7], Letter 131, p. 145.

faerie, is both a challenge and a call to arms to future fantasists. Tolkien's legacy to the genre is, I feel, as he would have wished. He is the piece of kindling that he aspired to be – the spark illuminating fantasy past, and inspiring fantasy yet to come.